Contents

For Charles and Ruthi Greer, the

Godparents of my two little girls,

on this first anniversary of Charles's passing.

Over many years, you have been as supportive of me

as two friends can be, and I could not have written this

book without you. Ruthi, my friend for twenty years,

you truly feel like my sister. You gave me the

encouragement and the means to write this book, and

I will always be grateful to both you and Charles.

All my love,

Franny
April 17, 2012

In 1979, I assumed that my life would finally settle into something approaching normal. I was frankly exhausted: In just a couple of years I had weathered the death of my beloved father, moved to Sin City, worked in a mob-fronted money-laundering operation, gotten divorced (and remarried, and re-divorced), had seen my son kidnapped, demolished a bar, practically killed a trollop in my own bed, and almost single-handedly opened a hotel. It turned out that these were just a prelude to an even more unbelievable period of my life.

—Franny Marcum

Me and Mom—

Me and Aubrey

Me and Jan

Aubrey in
front of our
house

Chapter One

LaFollette

"TIME TO GET UP," came first, called out by my sweet mother every morning of her life as she broke up kindling for the stove and fireplace. Once that was accomplished she retrieved that old black bread pan in which she baked biscuits for her family of nine. It would still be dark outside when we heard her shuffling about—it took a while to get the house warm. Should any of us seven kids dally, a more stern order came from our "old man," as we called him (just not to his face.) For me, it went like this:

"Black Cat, hit the floor!"

OK, I know it's a strange name for a cute little girl, but it was just one of a jillion things that I took for normal, only to find out years later how completely abnormal they all were. As for my name, I supposedly looked like my aunt, the original "Black Cat," who had jet-black hair and was quite the looker. It turned out that my real name was Frances Marcum (as I finally found out on my first day of elementary school) and the four-room Marcum family house that the old man—real name James—built sat precariously on a hillside that bordered a football field-sized, thirty-foot deep sinkhole.

LaFollette, TN—The City That Time Forgot

We were deep in the Cumberland Mountains, part of the Appalachian chain, forty miles or so northwest of Knoxville, Tennessee, and a short six-mile walk to the former coal town of LaFollette. But for a dirt-poor family with no car, those places were a universe away. Although I didn't know it at the time, folks like us existed in a time capsule that was stuck in the 19th century. LaFollette was a very small mountain town, where, since the coalmines had closed, very few men worked at all. Most of them did what my dad did: made whiskey or hung out in the poolroom, where women weren't allowed. The town had one of everything: one doctor, one dentist, one theater, one factory, one grocery, one elementary school, one high school, and one funeral home.

If there were rich people there I never knew of any. Nobody had a lot of money, but everybody somehow found a way to afford a lot of kids. When someone in your family died, the one funeral home cleaned them up and brought them back home, and you would sit up for three days and three nights with them. On the third day you buried them.

As I said, the Marcums were far from alone in their deprivations. I was reminded of this when I was about five years old and the family took one of its twice-a-year trips to Cas Walker's grocery store south of Knoxville. On this trip, Cas was out on the porch, speaking to a small crowd to see if any of them

Mrs. Ralston's second grade class—that's me in the front row, second from right. If I had to wear a dress, I still kept my jeans on

could help a local family in need. What had happened was that a family of fourteen who was even poorer than us, and lived in a *one*-room cabin in Locust Ridge, had just witnessed that home burn to the ground, along with all their possessions. Cas then brought out this blonde-haired little girl about my age who was wearing tattered overalls.

"This sweet little thing lost everything in that fire but her voice," Cas said. "And she would like to sing a song for you to thank you for helping her mommy and daddy and her brothers and sisters."

Then this girl sang a real fast mountain-style hillbilly song whose name escapes me, but I was impressed at how fast it was but yet how every word was still crystal clear. When the song ended, Cas spoke to the crowd again.

"This baby lost her only dress in that fire. Surely, some of you kind folks have an extra dress you can spare."

My heart was breaking for that girl, so I asked my mom: "Momma, can I please give that girl a dress."

"Black Cat, that's very sweet," mom answered, "but you only have one dress yourself. We'll give them some food instead."

I felt so bad for the Parton family, but that little girl Dolly ended up replacing that dress, and then some.

I thought everybody lived like this, though I would later learn that the entire outside world didn't know how Campbell County, Tennessee lived in the 1950s. But it worked both ways: I had no idea what extravagances existed beyond Appalachia, so I was never frustrated—I never knew what I was missing.

I was born in 1947, when both my parents were thirty years old, so my earliest clear memories are of the Fifties. But I'd bet that my recollections of that time are a lot different than yours, although we *did* have our own version of Happy Days. In addition to no electricity, the tiny house our father built for us also had no running water, plumbing, or heat—nothing but a roof, two stoves, and a path to the outhouse, which the old man rebuilt every two years. He was an electrician by day (ironic since the Marcum house didn't possess that luxury) and a moonshiner by night— never once caught by the agents of the Bureau of Internal Revenue, or "revenuers." But moonshine violence hit our family big time nonetheless.

On June 12, 1946, a year before I arrived on the scene, my

The Revenuers bust up a Tennessee moonshine operation

grandfather on my mother's side, Bob Stanford, and his two sons (my uncles Jay and Euliss, who were in one of John Dillinger's gangs), and a policeman named Drew Roberts, died in a moonshine territorial shootout in my granddad's restaurant, The LaFollette Café, downtown on Tennessee Avenue.[1] Fearing a clan war would erupt when my other uncles Cecil and Sterling sought revenge, my father took us to his hometown of Baltimore to hide out for a year or so. That's where they happened to be when I was born; otherwise, I would never have been born in a hospital.

Even though whisky had been legal since Prohibition was repealed in 1933, most southern hill folk still preferred the taste, not to mention the much higher alcohol content, of "white lightning," also known as moonshine. It had the additional advantage of being a miracle elixir, and many were the times I took it for a cold, a bad tooth, or rubbed it on an open cut. Of course, running hooch down nearby "Thunder Road" (Rt. 33, where NASCAR came into being) had dropped off, and, in order to make ends meet the younger locals grew pot. They were brilliant about it, planting their crops on TVA-owned property that they knew would never get raided. It just so happened that the Appalachian soil was so rich that that the weed grown there had twice the THC content as other kinds. Nevertheless, the old man stayed with his "shine."

As for my mother, the former Edna Stanford, she was like all the other women I saw in Campbell County, a housewife and

forty years. The inside is shown on the next page

mother first. And she had her work cut out for her; originally there were nine kids, but two passed away very young (of polio and pneumonia). I was pretty much in the middle, with two older brothers, three younger, and one younger sister. Anyway, after the kids were fed and sent walking off to school about an hour away,

---

[1] A local named Brazelle "Dynamite" Burkett spent a little time in jail for the shootout, but I was told that he was forced to "take the fall" for the real shooters.

my mom walked five miles every day, in all kinds of weather, to the Big Shirt Factory where she and practically every other

woman in town worked, but not before making sure we kids had plenty of chores lined up for when we got home. I'm not talking about doing dishes or mowing a lawn. Our assignments were much more basic to survival—things like gathering firewood, coal, water, and kindling. That was our after-school activity, and they started for me when I was six years old. Because I was a girl, it naturally fell to me to also take care of the younger babies. I was feeding them, washing them, and changing their diapers before I started elementary school.

We carried water into the house in two two-gallon buckets. We only had one dipper so we all drank out of it, and so did everyone else that came around. We had two stoves, the one in the kitchen we called the cook stove, which you had to keep a fire in all year round because we had to cook. The other was a potbellied stove in our parents' room, which managed to keep the house warm because we didn't have doors to the other rooms. As you can imagine, after-school sports teams and chess clubs didn't exist, at least not for the Marcum kids or most of our neighbors down the road.

The meals mom prepared for us consisted of whatever we could grow in the backyard. Red meat was a luxury, and we only had chicken on Sundays. Otherwise it was beans, potatoes, corn bread, apples, and whatever vegetables we grew in the garden. Instead of meat, we cooked a pot of pinto beans every day. We bought fifty-pound sacks of flour, meal, sugar, and a big canister of lard.

These would last most of the year. Almost everybody had a cow for

milk and butter, and if you didn't, you could buy it from your neighbor. Candy and other sweets were our Christmas presents; I never had a toy in my life. I only saw movies when mom "went tradin'" in LaFollette on some Saturdays (my parents were Cherokee descendants, and mom usually used the same terms the Indians used for centuries. Instead of shopping, they went tradin'.) Everybody went into town on Saturday to socialize or shop, and the stores would let you run a tab and pay when you could. The women would put their kids in the town's one movie theater, the Cherokee, on Saturday morning and we stayed there all day while our mothers did their shopping and their men were out getting

My hero, Lash LaRue

drunk. For the price of a 10-cent ticket, our parents had a daylong babysitter. Six or eight hours later us kids thought our eyes were going to fall out.

I often sat with my brothers in the Cherokee Theater,

Little Barb Sanders at the Tennessee Jamboree

watching cowboy movies with stars like Roy Rogers. I had a crush on Louisiana's Bogart look-alike, Lash LaRue. We never owned a television, so the most common form of entertainment was a battery-powered radio. On WLAF we listened to Barn Dance Radio shows and the Tennessee

Jamboree, where Bill Monroe, the Blue Valley Boys, and Little Barb Sanders were regulars. My personal favorite show was *Amos and Andy*.

One Appalachian tune that I loved was

The Blue Valley Boys at the Tennessee Jamboree

"Knoxville Girl" by the Blue Sky Boys. I guess it was about a young girl who lived not far from me here in Tennessee. It was the weirdest song because it had a melody that sounded like a nursery rhyme but the subject was the bloody murder of this poor girl by her boyfriend, and it was described in gory detail. Everybody sang it constantly, including me. Looking back now, I wonder if that song played a subconscious role in my general distrust of the male species.

As I lay every morning with three other kids in the same rollaway bed, waiting until the last possible minute, I fantasized about what I'd like to do that day. But it was always just that, a fantasy, because every day I'd have to clean this house and take care of the babies, of which there always seemed to be at least two in diapers. By the time I was in school, the old man had stopped working. He had gotten injured—I don't remember how—and now he stayed home, made whiskey, drank whiskey, and beat the hell out of any of us kids that got in his way. One way I managed to prevent beatings was to blackmail the old man. I'd find his gallon jug of 'shine and bury it. I'd go out and fetch him a glassful as long as he didn't beat me. I could also get him to do the dishes and other chores in exchange for a glass. Of course, when the hooch ran out he'd beat the daylights out of me—I couldn't figure out how to avoid that one. Mostly, I learned really young to just stay out of his way and keep my mouth shut, especially about anything concerning the family. On one occasion, that silence almost cost me my life. That adventure started in my version of a playground: the sinkhole.

My favorite thing to do as a child was to look for old whiskey bottles in the sinkhole (which was off limits to me), take them to the creek, rinse the mud off of them, and sell them to the bootleggers for a nickel a bottle. The sinkhole was straight across the lane from the house—in fact, all the neighbors built their houses around that thing. For kids, that off-limits crevice was like *The Lost World*; it was dark, with a lot of trees, grapevines, snakes— and a lot of whiskey bottles tossed in by people who would throw in their garbage and anything else they didn't want. But I loved it; I could hide up in trees, pretending I was somebody else.

Of course that dangerous pit would lead to many misadventures and beatings. My life-threatening incident came one day when I tripped on a root and fell into the pit, cutting myself bad; but I didn't tell anyone. We always had a lot of stitches and bruises, but no one got coddled or fussed over. And even though this cut was different I still couldn't fess up to how I got it, or even let anyone see it: I knew that the beating I would get from the old man would be a lot worse than the cut. My arm wouldn't move after the injury, but I wrapped it up tight and wore long sleeve shirts. It didn't hurt—I just couldn't use it anymore. After about a week, while I was over at the neighbor's picking apples, the neighbor lady noticed me working with just one hand.

"Black Cat, what's the matter with your arm?" she asked while walking over to have a closer look.

She took hold of me, pushed up my shirt, and unwrapped the bloody, dirty rag I had wrapped around it. She walked me back to my house, walking straight through the back door. My mom never knew what to expect with all of us kids, since one or more of us were always up to something. But when she saw the bloody rag and the neighbor lady, she knew this was serious. Somewhat in a panic, my mother, who was nursing one of those babies, came and looked at my arm.

"Oh, my God! We have to take her to a doctor," she said. She immediately stopped nursing, put the baby down and quickly got her things together for the long walk to the only local physician, old Doc Price. He was the kind of doctor who went to people's houses, and he knew all of us kids because he and the neighbor lady helped my mom have all of her babies, right there in the house—I was the only one delivered in a hospital.

My uncle was visiting at the time, and he picked me up quickly.

"Come on, Edna, I'll go with you," he said. "It's about six miles into town."

That was quite a walk. By the time we got to the doctor's

office, I was scared, not because of the cut on my arm, but because my mom was badgering me about how this had happened. I couldn't tell her that I had been in the sinkhole looking for whiskey bottles. She would kill me, and the old man would kill me even worse.

"I fell on a piece of glass," I said.

I never did tell her where it happened. I'll take that one to my grave, I thought at the time. My mom, uncle, and the neighbor lady all plunged into the doctor's little office with me in tow. Of course Doctor Price knew who we all were and immediately put me on his table to look at the cut.

"Oh, my God, what happened?"

"I fell on a piece of glass," I repeated.

"I need more people in here to hold her down," Doctor Price said. "Go get three more people off the street. Edna, she's cut her leader [tendon] in two. It's about up to her elbow. I'm going to see if I can go through the wound, up her arm, and pull it back down and tie it in a knot. How old is this cut?"

Everyone looked at me. I replied, "Six days." Again I heard the doctor exclaim, "Oh, my God! If I can't get the leader back down and tied, she will lose the use of this arm."

What the hell does that mean? My uncle hurried outside and came back with three total strangers, and *the fight was on!* I had six adult people holding me down—my legs, arms, head, and chest, but I could still see something that looked like a pair of foot-long tweezers in the doctor's hand. I screamed so loud you probably could hear me a mile away. I repeated all those bad words I heard my dad say when he was mad. I don't know how long this took, but it was dark outside when we began to walk back home. I was all bandaged up, with sixty-eight stitches in my right arm. It hurt more now than it did when it happened. Well, to make a long story short, the arm got better, but I have a very ugly scar. I didn't mind then, and never have.

The summers seemed really long back then, but they weren't summer vacations like kids have today, because there was still plenty of work that had to be done. Still, I was content because I thought the rest of the world lived the same way. I only learned differently when I was ten and we traveled up to Detroit to visit relatives who were having a big outdoor barbecue. It was my first time away from LaFollette.

The first thing that confused me about the big city was my Uncle Cecil's "inside bathroom."

"Black Cat, how do you like it here?" he asked me over hot dogs around the picnic table.

"I don't understand, uncle," I answered. "You guys eat outside and shit inside. Back in Tennessee we do just the opposite."

Needless to say, he thought that was funny, but understandable coming from someone that had never been out of the mountains. And my habit of saying unintentionally funny things was just beginning—I have no idea where that trait came from. My uncle also had an "inside television." Wow! I was astonished to see such a thing. The only television set I had ever seen belonged to the old man and woman that lived at the end of the lane. They would put it on the front porch in the evenings and all us kids got to sit in the yard under a big tree and watch this new invention. They shared it with the whole neighborhood, so I just thought they were supposed to be on the porch. Like the "inside outhouse," I was so fascinated by this contraption that I was content just staring at the test patterns on it. That was the beginning of this high technology boom and it hasn't slowed down since.

My parents finally moved down the lane from the house my dad built, the only home I had ever known. The new place also had one of those fancy inside outhouses—what was the world coming to? The first day there I spent hours flushing the water, then running outside, crawling up under the floor to see where the water was going. But I never could figure it out. When the old man came home, I told him what I was doing all day. Boy, was he mad: "Black Cat, you dumb ass, that's now city water, and I have to pay for it. Keep your damn hands off that."

Electricity? Wow again. Now, all you had to do was pull a string and you had light. No more buying coal oil. You also had two little holes in the wall to make things work. One day the old man brought home a thing called a "hot plate," and my older brother, Junior, stuck these two thin prongs in the wall and that thing turned a bright orange. Again I was amazed. I asked him, "Is that hot?" He said no, so I proceeded to lay my entire hand on this bright orange round thing, which burned my hand until it looked like a burned pork chop. He got a beating for that one.

The old man could be a bastard. I remember that because, since the new place had electricity, we finally acquired a beat-up old tube television set, and he guarded it like a mother hawk over her hatchlings. Basically, we were only allowed to watch it when the old man watched it, and we only watched what he watched. It was impossible to sneak a peek when he was gone because that old cuss took out one of the tubes and put it in his pocket every time he left. He said the television would distract us from doing our chores. (I wish the old man was around today to take the tubes out my grandson's computer, but that's another story.)

From my diary:

As I lay on a flat rock watching ants crawl all around me and the sun beating down on me, my back and legs were still stinging from the belt my father had used on me. This was another day like many days before when he had went into a rage.

I could hear his footsteps getting closer, and my heart pounding harder: If he finds me he will kill me for sure for running from him.

He didn't always get this drunk, but today was different. I usually could take the whippings knowing they would soon be over, but this day I didn't think he would ever stop.

When he let loose of my arm I ran and ran until I could hear my heart making more noise than my bare feet on the gravel road. I remembered some high weeds and a big flat rock hid among the thorny bushes.

I lay there, so quiet 'til I could no longer hear his footsteps. I barely raised my head to see where he was, and I could see him staggering back to our house. I lay back down and took a deep breath and soon fell asleep.

Another major chore was planting a garden. Some years we could afford to have the garden plowed by an old neighbor man and his mule, but more often my dad and my two older brothers did it all with a spading fork, taking turns one row at a time until all the dirt had been turned over. One year my older brother drove that spading fork all the way through his foot. Again, no sympathy there from the old man. He was just told how stupid he was and how he doubled the work for the rest of us. The old man poured the wounds full of white lightning—he said it killed germs. On top of that he poured salt, and wrapped it up. And nothing else was to be said about it—no crying and no limping.

The garden would feed us all winter. The old man did the canning while my mother was at work at the shirt factory. I stood on a chair and watched every move the old man made. But we kids also helped. My job was washing all those canning jars. I loved having a garden, especially because I could hide in the cornfields, pretending I was in a jungle like I seen in a *Tarzan* movie. Of course, I was "Jane." I carried an old plastic saltshaker with me, since my idea of going to dinner was heading off into the garden with that saltshaker and emptying it on a fresh-picked piece of corn or whatever else looked ripe. It was dirty, but it worked. But back then I had never heard of the word "lunch." We had breakfast, dinner, and supper.

Everyone in our family had different and colorful personalities, but I must say it was a very good-looking bunch. I always felt that it's because of our pure Cherokee Indian blood— it had not been mixed like *Heinz 57*. We get it from both sides. Of course, the downside was that I quickly learned why it was illegal to give Indians whiskey. I had two older brothers, named Ralph and Junior, and these boys were always in trouble. Junior was the mastermind behind most all of our shenanigans, and he taught me a lot. Ralph was the tattletale, but only to mom because he didn't like how the old man beat us. We didn't get by with much because everybody knew everyone else's kids, and they would come right to the front door and tell on you.

We had an old preacher man in the neighborhood who was always scaring us kids into being good and telling us to come to church. He had the kind of church in which you had to handle snakes, speak in tongues, and put your hand in a jar of coal oil while it was flaming, then roll all over the floor like you were having a seizure. My mother told us to stay away from there, but Junior and I were fascinated with the actions of these people. One day Junior and Ralph were playing marbles in the front yard and happened to look up and saw the old preacher man coming down the lane. He had to be coming to our house because we were the only one that had a lane to it. Ralph jumped up, ran into the house and hid. He did not like getting chewed out by anyone. Meanwhile, Junior stood there like a beer can on a fence post. And sure enough the old preacher man had come to ruin their day. He told Junior what a bad boy he was, pointing his finger in his face. He told him that he had lost the Lord and that's why he was doing all these bad things.

"You're a lost young man and you have also lost the Lord, Jesus Christ!"

Junior didn't say a word—he didn't talk much anyway. Before the old preacher man left, he put both of his hands on Junior's head and shook him, saying in a loud voice, "The Lord is missing and you need to find him!"

Junior stood there like he was deaf and dumb, until the old preacher man left to go on his way. As soon as his back was turned, Junior took off into the house, where Ralph was hiding in the closet. Junior yanked the door open, panicked.

"Ralph get out of there, the Lord is missing and they think we had something to do with it!"

I don't know if he ever understood what was really going on. I know it took me a few years.

Junior's nickname was "Hard Rock," or "Rock House." That's what everybody called him because he always "rocked" anybody that pissed him off, like the guy that ran over his dog. Junior ran after him, popping the car with rocks, but the guy didn't even stop. Junior cried for days over that dog. As the years went by, Junior became a real cock hound, as my dad would say—a ladies man. All my friends thought he was so good-looking, which was true, but he was also a bad boy. Once he stole a whole tray full of rings from the five-and-ten-cent store, then gave one to every girl he knew. He got pinched for that one, and it ended up getting him locked up in a reform school. That place was like a prison for young bad boys, and they got a beating every day until the guards felt like they had broken their spirit. Junior said they made him bend over and grab his ankles while they beat him with a wet leather strap. But he was stubborn and tried fighting back, which only increased his time. My heart was broken, but when he did get out, he got drafted, which I thought might be a good thing for him. It was the beginning of the Vietnam War.

While Junior was in the reform school I got my first job, as a 12-year-old waitress at one of the curb service drive-in restaurants. I sat in front of that place, waiting for a car to pull up, then go to the driver's side and ask, "Can I help you?" I'd write down the order and then holler the order through the little square window. Then the cook handed it out the window and I'd take it to the car. For a day's work I was paid about three dollars (in cash!) On a good day I would make two more dollars in tips, but I had to split it with the cook.

For over a year I saved every penny so that I could buy a folk guitar. As I recall, it was a nice blonde guitar that cost me fifty dollars. That guitar was far and away the most valuable thing I ever owned, and I made sure that the other kids didn't get near it by hiding under my parents' bed. One of our kind neighbors regularly sat me down and showed me how to play it. I hoped that soon I would be joining in on the front porch jam sessions. But it wasn't meant to be. My soldier brother made sure of that, even if it was by accident. It all started when he fell in love with my best girlfriend.

When Junior was discharged, he married Carol, who was fourteen, just like me. She was from a big city in Ohio, and was quite the looker, with a body like Marilyn Monroe. I was still skinny, no figure. I looked like a twelve-year old boy. Carol tried to teach me about make-up and hair but it never turned out right. She shaved off all my eyebrows, drew them back on with a pencil, cut my hair, tried bleaching it, and put some bright red lipstick on me. All this was to make me look older so some boy might look at me. I ended up looking like a young rooster. The old man saw me, grabbed me by the hair, took his hand and rubbed hard on my face. Then he threw me to the side and yelled, "Black Cat, go wash your face and get all that whore wax off. Never let me see you looking like that again!" Was I that pretty or that ugly?

Because the new couple didn't have another place to live, they moved in with us and got the only private bedroom, a gift from my parents. But that meant that the other eight of us now all slept in the same tiny room, on mattresses, sofas and floors. Well, on their wedding night, Junior hightailed it into the bedroom, anxious to do whatever newlyweds do—neither Carol nor I knew anything about sex, so she was terrified and hid in the bathroom with me for an hour as we both tried to figure out what was going to happen. Eventually Carol joined Junior, and apparently he knew exactly what to do, and he did it with the force of a locomotive. I know that not only because we could hear it in the next room, but also because the next morning, when I went in to retrieve my precious guitar, I found it in fifty pieces under that spring mattress. My dreams of playing music were dashed, and I never revisited them. I just assumed it wasn't meant to be.

Junior and Carol made the move to Grand Rapids, Michigan, where I had my Uncle Cecil and Aunt Jean and all the cousins that I loved dearly. When school let out that year I talked my mom into letting me go up North with Junior and his new child bride, just for summer because mom needed me at home to help with the kids. (Oh, how I hated it every time she got pregnant. I cried whenever she made the announcement.) Cousin Iris was close to my age, and my favorite cousin. She had come down to Tennessee to visit me some summers, but this was the first time for me to spend time with her in a big city.

Well, not long after we arrived, Junior got us an upstairs apartment for twenty dollars a week in one of those old Victorian looking houses. While Junior went to work, Carol and I stayed home and giggled the same way we did before she married my brother. We were just fourteen, but thinking we were adults with all this newfound freedom. We kept the radio blasting all day while we listened to rock n' roll, danced to Elvis, Jerry Lee Lewis, and many more. Life was good even though we had no money. Junior only made about fifty bucks a week, but that was still more money than we had ever seen. As time went on, I thought I would like to make some money to help us out, so I decided I would get a job. At fourteen, I didn't know how to do anything, but I was never afraid to try. There was a Bob's Big Boy a few blocks away and I knew I could do curb service because I had worked at that drive-in restaurant back in Tennessee. So this Bob's Big Boy can't be that much different (I thought). It would just be another curbside service.

I talked Carol into going with me to get the job and we walked and giggled all the way. We arrived at this restaurant, and I had never seen so many cars in one place. Carol asked a waitress if we could see the manager. We waited, and soon a huge man came out, saying, "Come in here, young ladies." He had an office with a big desk, and we sat in two chairs across from him.

"Who needs a job?"

"I do!" I immediately replied.

"Have you had experience?"

"Yes sir!"

"How old are you?

"Sixteen," I lied.

"I need for you to fill out an application."

I looked at Carol, thinking, "What the hell is that?" I didn't know what he was talking about, but he slid a long yellow piece of paper across his desk: "Fill this out, come out and get me when you finish. I need to be back on the floor."

I read it—it was asking my name and address, that kind of stuff. As I got further down the "application," I didn't understand why it had all these personal questions. For instance: "SEX:" Why do they need to know this? I just chalked it up as big city ways, but

I answered it. I wrote "Never." I didn't want him to think I was a bad girl, and I wasn't. Farther down the page it asked me if I had a hernia. What the hell is that? I wrote, "Yes." I thought the more questions you answered "yes" to, the better off you were.

Finally I finished, so I asked Carol to find this manager guy to tell him I was through. He came back into his office and sat down and began to read this "application" thing. He was smirking, trying not to laugh. So I thought, "He likes me and he'll give me a job." He looked me straight in the eye.

"So you have a hernia?"

"Yes sir," I replied proudly.

"Where is it located?"

"Back in Tennessee," I replied.

The manager keeled over in his chair laughing hysterically, and so did Carol. I sat there bewildered, waiting for someone to share the laughter with me. When this manager finally could get his breath, he said, "Young lady, I don't think you're ready for a job."

I got up and walked out of his office mad, thinking, "You dumb-ass Yankee." When we got outside the place, Carol was still laughing.

"I can't believe you said that," she said.

"What did I say?"

"You said you had a hernia."

"So, what's so funny about that?"

"You said it was back in Tennessee."

She was laughing so hard she began to piss her pants—really. Now I think *that's* funny, so I began to laugh at *her*. When we got back home, the more mature 19-year-old Junior, who normally didn't share our sense of humor, was there. He looked real mean at us: "Where have you two been?" Carol answered immediately because he was a jealous man and she'd better have a good answer: "We went to get Franny a job, and you won't believe what this damn idiot said!" Carol began to tell the story and even Junior started laughing hysterically.

"So what the hell is a hernia?" I asked.

"That's when your guts fall out of your ass," he answered through his laughter.

I tried to visualize this because I knew what guts looked like. I had seen enough slaughtered animals as a kid—but never human guts. I visualized these guts dragging behind me while I was trying to walk. I never knew anyone with that kind of ailment. Carol starts screaming in laughter even more, continuing to piss all over the place.

"No, Junior, that's hemorrhoids," she said. "You're as mixed up as Black Cat."

But from then to now I have never had to fill out another one of them "applications."

My Aunt Jeanie worked in a bakery across from the Bob's Big Boy parking lot, and she offered to try and get me some work there. If it hadn't been for her giving us bread and rolls that were a day old we would have starved to death. One day she stopped by our place to check on us and bring more food. I can still see her trying to climb the stairs, with those pink boxes full of goodies. God bless her—she had nine kids and was pregnant with another one.

I returned back to the mountains again at summer's end, since I had to go back to school, which I actually looked forward to. I always had lots of friends who were much more physically developed than me, but I kept everybody laughing. However, I was sometimes the brunt of a lot of my own jokes.

My best friend as a child was Dianna. We had a lot in common, especially the fact that we both had a parent who drank and beat the hell out of us just for existing. But we could be honest with each other; we didn't want anyone else knowing what our home life was like. It wasn't long before Dianna got married also. All of my friends seem to be getting married, having kids, and dropping out of school. If there were twenty girls in my freshmen high school class, there were only four left by graduation. But your friends aren't the same after they get married because then

Me at sixteen—my last year in school

they have to do what their husbands tell them to do—total bullshit in my eyes. I finally bit the bullet when I was sixteen, an old maid in Campbell County.

I married the first person that asked me, and it happened to be a big mistake. The only reason I got married was because now I would be able to stay out past ten o'clock and do what I wanted to—no more mom telling me what to do and getting beaten by the old man for not doing it. But I was too young, too much of a free spirit, and a rebel against anybody telling me what to do. I remember on the day I got married, my oldest brother saw the wedding dress (no gown) lying on the bed. He asked me, and I told him I was getting married. He said the only place I will wear that dress is in my coffin. He hated the idea of me getting married not only because of my age but because it wasn't what he wanted for me in life. We fought all over the house, my poor mother trying to break it up. Now I was more determined than ever because I saw this as my way out. I got dressed after taking a hell of a beating from my brother, and of course I made it worse by fighting back, but that's just who I am.

I got married at the local funeral parlor because the guy who ran it was also a Justice of the Peace. I knew him well because when I worked curb service as a kid, he was one of my customers and I had to deliver his dinners to the funeral home. One night he showed me the room where they worked on dead people—it looked like an operating room. I never wanted to see that again and I wished later that I had never seen it in the first place! Little did I know I would soon be married there. Now that I think about it, it was actually quite appropriate, given how that marriage went. In short, women were not well treated in that world. To give you an idea of how women were perceived in 1950s Campbell County, my wedding gift from my parents was a washboard. For reasons that aren't quite clear even to me, I kept that thing until the present day. I guess it reminds me of what a crazy life I've lived and how it all started. It also tells me that we can rise above what other people say your lot in life is.

My new husband, Dan, was a few years older than me—not much, but old enough to go into bars where I wasn't allowed. Needless to say, this caused a lot of fights, physical fights. This marriage thing was not what I thought it was supposed to be. Anyway, after the funeral home "wedding," he took me straight to his parents' house to stay. He was the oldest boy among twelve brothers and sisters. The first week he left to go up North to Detroit to get work, and he told me to stay put and not to leave the house, that he'd be back soon to get me. After two days I began to feel really uncomfortable around these people, so I decided to take the car and go to my mother's. As all of Dan's brothers watched me put my clothes in the car, one decided to let the air out of all four tires.

Boy, was I pissed now! I got a neighbor to help me get the tires pumped back up, and just as I was ready to pull out, one of his brothers stood in front of the car and told me that I wasn't leaving because his brother had told him to keep an eye on me. Sitting in the car, motor running, I replied, "I'm only going to tell you once to move, then if I have to again, I'm going to run over your ass."

He stood there defiantly, so I gunned it, and he flipped up on the hood. I made a quick turn and slung him off, never looking back—I didn't give a damn if he was dead. It wasn't long after I was at my mother's house that the police knocked on the door. This cop, Willie, whom I had known all my life, was about seven feet tall—or he at least seemed that large to a smallish sixteen-year-old illegal driver. I hadn't told my mother and father about the incident because I just assumed that it would only make things worse (it did).

"Black Cat, I have a serious complaint on you," Willie said. "Did you run over your husband's brother today?"

"Yes sir, is he dead?"

"No," said Willie, "but he's pretty bruised up. Was this an accident?"

"No," I replied. I told him what happened, that I had given him a warning to move but he chose not to.

"You should have called us," he said.

"I'm sixteen," I said, "so if they press charges on me, I will press charges for kidnapping. I have that right, don't I?"

"Let me see if I can get this straightened out," Willie said, somewhat dazed. "I'll get back with you." That was the last I ever heard of it. I was never liked very much after that, but I didn't care. Nobody does something to me and gets by with it. An eye for an eye, as the old man would say.

Jan was my only sister, and my only ally against all those boys. She's seven years younger than me and so beautiful; everybody said so from the time she was born. I was there for that too. My mom had her at home, like all the others. It was in the middle of the night, and the old man was out of town working. I remember hearing her saying softly, "Black Cat?"

My eyes immediately opened and I went straight to her.

"I need for you to go to the neighbor's," mom said, "and ask if you can use their phone. Call Doctor Price and tell him who you are, give him my name and say that I need him to come here as quickly as possible."

Off I went into the dark, running as fast as I could to the neighbor's, where I beat on their door with all I had. The door opened, and I can still see Miss Bailey standing there with that chenille housecoat on.

"My mom needs help," I cried. "Can I use your phone to call the doctor?"

"I'll call him," she said. "Wait for me and I'll walk you back home." Back at the house I was told to stay in the kitchen, keep the fire going and heat some water. I don't remember this, but my mom always told this story about when I came into the room where the doctor was holding my sister up by her feet and smacking her.

"Look, Black Cat," he said, "you now have a little sister." Apparently, I wasn't impressed.

"Hit her again," I replied. "She shouldn't have crawled up there in the first place."

The neighbor lady took Baby Janice (we called her Jan) into

the kitchen, and I watched her clean her up and wrap her in an Indian blanket. She said, "Black Cat, sit down here by the stove and keep the baby warm, I have to take care of your mother."

Wow, Jan grew up to be beautiful, smart, and sweet, not like me. She also married really young, at seventeen, right after she graduated. Her thirty-seven-year-old husband, JR, had been my softball coach when I was fourteen. He divorced his wife, abandoned his two young kids, and married this beautiful, young maiden, and was extremely jealous of her. A handsome man with lots of girls vying for his attention, JR owned a bar that his new wife wasn't even old enough to enter. I remember once when my husband, a couple of my brothers, and their wives were sitting at a big round table in a bar, and a girl walked up to the table using some bad language. I, of course, had to call her on it. Somebody at the table whispered in my ear that she was after my sister's husband. Now that really made my blood boil, since she was nothing but a bar tramp anyway, and I knew my sister spent a lot of nights home crying and wondering where her husband was.

Again she let out some filthy talk. I stood up from the table, warned her again about talking filthy in front of my husband and my brothers. She said, "Sit down, bitch, before you get hurt." I looked at her with rage. When I saw there was a five-foot fan behind her, I shoved her into it and held her there 'til the fan sucked in her long hair. Now she couldn't move, with her hair twisted in the fan blades up to her scalp. I beat her face until I couldn't see her eyes anymore. (I remembered what the old man once said: if you get them down, you never let them back up). There was lots of blood, but she needed to be taught a lesson. I had no mercy on her, and by the time someone unplugged the fan and pulled me away she wasn't talking anymore.

I went out and sat down in my husband's car while the ambulance carried her out. My older brother, whom I fought with a lot, came out and said to me: "Well, Black Cat, you've done it now. She's dead." That didn't scare me, I still wanted more of her—she hurt my baby sister. Then my husband came out, jumped into the car, and drove off with me.

"Are you crazy?" he yelled at me.

"She asked for it," I said.

He took me to my mom's and said, "Get out! I don't want to be around when they arrest you." I called him a fucking coward and many more names that I thought he deserved. He left me there at the side of the road all alone. I went into my mom's house but I didn't tell her anything, not wanting to worry her. Soon some friends came by and blew the horn. I went outside and they told me what was going on in town. They told me that the bitch was in the hospital. She's not dead? My friends said no and started laughing. I told them what my older brother had said. They laughed again. "He just wanted to scare you," one of them said. She got out of the hospital and didn't press charges; it was chalked up to a barroom brawl. But I found out later that the owner of the bar said I couldn't come back in there because this woman happened to be one of his girlfriends. I sent word that she better not go back into my brother-in-law's bar, or next time it would be worse.

What with me raising hell in town and my new husband desperate for work in a place where most men just boozed it up, it seemed like the time was right to leave the only world I had ever known. Little did I know that my crazy adventures in LaFollette would be nothing compared to those I'd have in the outside world. I had never experienced life in a big city, and I sure as hell know that the big cities had never experienced anyone like Franny Marcum.

Chapter Two

Goodbye Appalachia, Hello World

DAN AND I EVENTUALLY MOVED two-hundred-and-fifty miles away to Atlanta, Georgia, where it would be easier for him to find painting and construction jobs. He found work, but he also found women. For me, it was a dark time in an otherwise happy, carefree life. Dan was always stepping out on me, which led to some terribly physical fights. But even though I was a hardheaded woman who took no guff from anyone, I stayed with him. Divorce just wasn't a choice in those days, especially after we had our first child, Travis, in 1971. I really wanted to hold the family together for him, but deep down I knew it couldn't last. Life had suddenly gotten so complicated that I actually missed gardening with the old man and playing in that sinkhole. My childhood had such a hold on me that I made Dan drive us back to Campbell County every weekend—five hours each way.

In April 1975 I was still living a lie in Atlanta when I received the worst news of my life: the old man had died. I was later told that I reacted by taking off running and screaming, "This can't be true! My dad is too tough to die!" Before I knew anything, I was back in LaFollette—I didn't even remember how I got there, although I now know that Dan took me there with baby Travis. I expected to see my father when I got home, but I never did. Apparently, there wasn't much left to see. No one told me how he died until I got there, but it turned out that it all started when mom and dad moved away from the countryside.

My mom had always wanted to live closer to downtown, and another family tragedy finally made that move possible. My dad's brother had a house with a barbershop in front at the edge of town. Every room had a fireplace, even the barbershop. One morning, dad went down to the shop to visit, like he did every day, and found his brother dead in his bedroom. He had spread out newspapers all over the floor, laid down on them, then put a gun to his head and pulled the trigger. No one ever knew why. Of course, the house went to dad, so he and the boys cleaned it up, and mom and dad moved in. The old man took his brother's room—he wasn't afraid of anything. He preferred that room because he could sneak his moonshine in without my mom seeing it. It was the very same room my dad would die in.

As best we could tell, one night while the rest of the family was out, the old man was smoking a cigarette when he fell asleep in his brother's old room, burning the entire house down with him in it. My little brothers and sister and my mom came back from the store to find out that everything they owned had gone up in flames, including most of our precious family mementos and photos. They couldn't get my dad out until the house stopped burning. That's why they wouldn't let me see him. But when you don't see the body, it's harder to believe the person is really gone. How do I know if it's true if I can't see him? I went to the funeral home, but they told me no, it wouldn't help things. I begged them. I even got so mad that they had to drag me away kicking and screaming.

No matter how hard they tried to make me believe the old man was gone, I just couldn't. My mind was still seeing him; my head was still hearing him and all the funny things he said to try to calm down my childhood fears and insecurities. For instance, I was always asking about why I was so short, until he finally explained, "Black Cat, you're not short, they just built the street too close to your ass." When I was very young, I had an unnatural fear of dying—I guess it was a stage I was going through—and I can remember talking about it all the time, often on these field trips. So one day when I was bugging the old man about it for the umpteenth time, he said to me, "Black Cat, you'll have to be hit in the head with a hammer on judgment day, now quit thinking about this stuff."

All the things he had taught me played over and over in my brain like a broken record, some of it handed down from our Cherokee ancestors, and some from hill folk moonshiners. One of my favorite things to hear him say was, "Hit the floor, Black Cat, we're going blackberry pickin' today." When we walked through the fields, crossing the creeks to find those blackberries in the beautiful early morning daylight, he taught me so many things along the way. He showed me different roots and what we could use them for. For instance, you can boil "cat nip," strain it through a cloth, add some white syrup, and give it to babies that have colic. I did this for Travis. He taught me how to pick pokeweed, and how long to boil it in a mixture of lard and salt—you have to boil it a long time or it can be poisonous. After it cooled down it became "polk salad," and it tasted great with corn bread. It also had some healing properties; our Cherokee ancestors used it for everything from infections to boils. We also picked mint on these walks, then later we boiled it and made tea; this was good for a cold.

I remember him showing me how to deal with other injuries, like snakebites. "Black Cat," he said, "if you get a snake bite, tie this rubber tube above the bite. It slows down the blood flow. Then take your knife and cut a X on the bite—sometimes you might have to suck on it real hard, but make sure you spit it out." I never had to do this, but I know how. On future hikes I always carried a little box that held a knife, a rubber tube, and a suction cup.

Then there were the words of wisdom which I'm sure had nothing to do with our Cherokee ancestors, but they had a kernel of truth them nonetheless, and I passed them on to my own kids.

1. Opinions are like assholes—everybody has one.
2. Information is ammunition.
3. Don't talk if it's not necessary.
4. You have two ears and one mouth, so listen twice as much as you talk.
5. I'm too old of a cat to be clawed up by a kitten.
6. You must never fear the face of no man or the ass of no woman.[2]

There were so many things I learned from him, but now it was if those days had burned to the ground and turned to ash along with the house.

After the fire, we stayed in Tennessee to help mom find a new place to live. I wanted to be with her while she got accustomed to her life without her husband, then I rented a small place nearby, not sure if I wanted to return to Atlanta. But eventually I did, and my sister and her husband joined me. Not long after returning to Atlanta, Jan ended up with a one of those

---

[2] A couple others that I can't forget: "Black Cat, quit eating so much cheese or I'll have to put a screen on your ass to keep the rats out," and "My luck is so bad, if there was a crack going to Hell, I would lose weight and fall through it."

Barbizon modeling contracts. One day in February she stopped by the house while I was outside chopping wood—my husband was (typically) down at the poolroom, or off with his friends. Having a young child didn't change him one whit. Watching my blistered hands bleed, Jan sat on a stump, crying.

"I can't stand to see you doing stuff like this," she said.

"If I don't keep the house warm my baby will freeze to death," I explained.

I continued chopping wood while she told me that she and her husband were leaving for Los Angeles to follow-up on this modeling contract. I was so happy for her.

"You need to leave this town," she said, "and maybe your husband will make a better life for you if he's away from all of his buddies."

We hugged and cried together. "Someday I'll get you away from all of this," Jan said before driving off. Four days later she called me and said she was in Las Vegas, Nevada. They never even made it to California.

"We're going to stay here," she explained. "My husband can work and there's plenty of modeling jobs. Please come here."

When we hung up the phone, my heart yearned to be with her. I didn't like the thought of her being alone with him. Although I loved him to death, I knew he could get violent with her over his jealousy. I waited for my husband Dan to come home so I could talk to him about it, but of course it was another one of those nights when he didn't show up. The next morning, furious, I thought to myself, I'm not going to fight with him anymore. He wandered in about seven that morning, only to clean up and leave again. I didn't say anything about my conversation with my sister: I had already made up my mind as to what I was going to do.

While he was gone, I sold everything in the house for five hundred dollars and walked to a neighbor's home to drop off Baby Travis. Then I had someone take me to Dan because I needed his car, which was new. Sure enough, the first beer joint I went to, he was there. But I didn't go in—I had the extra set of keys, and all I wanted was the car. I got in and off I went, back to pick up my baby at my mother's house. I was going to join my sister in Las Vegas.

Before I left the next morning, Dan showed up. I had just loaded Travis, my washboard-wedding gift, and our one suitcase in the trunk, when he came up running to the house out of breath.

"I'm comin' with you," he said. I suppose I had cooled down somewhat from the night before, and combined with my desire for Travis to have a father, I let him come along. But there was no way I was going to stay in Atlanta or go back to Campbell County. I wanted to go somewhere where the men weren't constantly tempted by booze and women. The fact that we went to Las Vegas tells a lot about what I knew of the outside world.

My strongest memory of the two-day drive to Las Vegas was how little four-year-old Travis stood between us in the front seat (back when cars had those bench seats) and would talk for hours on end, his mouth right at our ear levels. We pulled over five or six times so that Dan and I could step outside and have a smoke break, but what we were really doing was giving our ears a rest from Travis's high-pitched squealing.

Arriving in Las Vegas was like landing on another planet. I knew this place was weird as soon as I saw mountains with no trees, and the downtown main drag looked nothing like the one in LaFollette, or even big city Atlanta. It had so many people running around, up and down The Strip, and millions of lights. I was in awe.

This was the first time I saw mountains without trees

The year was 1975 and I was a twenty-seven year old firecracker who had unwittingly relocated to the most outrageous city in America. It was like mixing gasoline and matches, only I didn't know it yet. However, I knew right away this was no LaFollette.

Las Vegas is where I went into my first giant supermarket, and I was immediately confused at seeing bottled water on the shelf, where a sign said: "Drinking Water." I just assumed they gave away drinking water in bottles as opposed to in buckets. I approached the store manager.

"Why is water in bottles on the shelves? Is it free to take?"

"No!" he replied! "It's fifty-cents a gallon."

"Why? Why are you selling water? I've never heard of such a thing."

"Where you from?" he asked.

"LaFollette, Tennessee, and you don't have to pay for water there."

"Well, here the water is hard, so you can't drink it," he explained—sort of.

I couldn't understand what he meant by "hard water." It made no sense to me, so I didn't buy it because I thought it was a scam. What kind of people are these? I had seen a lot of hustlers back in Tennessee, but none of them was ever stupid enough to try to sell water. I eventually learned about hard water when I washed my first batch of clothes.

Jan and her husband had rented a small weekly apartment, and of course we stayed with them. Our husbands found work immediately, and I was a happy camper—at least at first. For the first time in my life I didn't have to build a fire to cook, or carry buckets of drinking water. I thought it odd that they had an easier time getting water here in the desert than we did in Campbell County. But now our husbands were gone even more, while my sister, myself, and Travis were cooped up in this little place with nowhere to go and nothing to do. I didn't hate Las Vegas; I hated my husband for not giving me any of the money he made gambling, and for going out gambling every night in the first place.

I remember having no money on our first Thanksgiving Day in Las Vegas. Jan and I cooked up some hot dogs and fried potatoes—that's all we had. When our husbands came home, they sat down and ate like it was no big deal, laughing and talking about their adventures in the casinos. I was getting madder and madder, and when I hit my boiling point I walked behind my husband, picked up Travis's chocolate milk, poured it over Dan's head, grabbed a fork and stabbed him in the back. When Jan saw the fork sticking out of Dan's back she freaked out.

"Oh, Black Cat, what have you done now?" she screamed.

"He's lucky it wasn't a knife," I said.

They pulled it out, cleaned him up, and, just like back in LaFollette, the fight was on! When we ran out of gas I told him that he'd better find us a place to live or I would take Travis and start walking back to Tennessee. He eventually got us a two-bedroom place in the new Barcelona Apartments in the center of town, but he was still staying out at night, drinking, gambling, and God knows what else.

I decided to get a job even though Dan didn't want me to work; I was tired of doing without. We lived near West Sahara Avenue, not far from The Strip, so I started walking, going into every place I thought might hire me. On the 500 block of East Sahara, I went into a dress shop that hadn't opened yet—they were still putting carpet down. A beautiful young girl was in there telling people what to do, so I walked up to her and I told her I was looking for work, that I was new in town and needed a job. To my surprise, I got the job and went to work a week later. Of all the thousands of local businesses I could have walked into for a job, I happened to pick the one that threw me right smack dab into center of the of the legendary Las Vegas-organized crime world. My knack for stumbling into craziness was not left behind in Tennessee, that's for sure.

I thought it was odd that everyone involved in this shop was from Chicago. In fact, Chicagoans were all over the neighborhood, along with New Yorkers—hardly anyone was actually from Las Vegas. Very strange. In LaFollette, *everyone* was from LaFollette. Rose, the manager brought out from Chicago by the owner, Lisa, was a lot older than me, so she showed me the ropes, and I caught on fast. Rose was a tough old broad, but she liked me a lot so we spent a lot of time together talking. Rose told me that Lisa, also from Chicago, had inherited twenty-five million dollars when she turned twenty-one. She said that her own father worked for a Chicago bootlegger named Al Capone, and she told me stories about Capone coming to her house all the time when she was very young. I told her about my old man, and how he sold white lightning in Campbell County during Prohibition, but nowhere near as successfully as this Capone guy, from what Rose said. It didn't take long before I realized who really ran this city; it was just like LaFollette, but on a *much* bigger scale. Having dealt with hustlers all our lives, Rose and I both understood the code of silence. This understanding that I was sort of born with would soon make me invaluable to the "boys from Chicago."

Now this dress shop was very fancy, featuring high-end clothing from all the well-known designers. Many of the Strip's entertainers did their shopping there (Totie Fields, Tina Turner etc.), as well as all of the top showgirls; they would come in and drop a thousand dollars like it was nothing. We also had a lot of wiseguys—always from Chicago—drop in, and Rose knew them all. Lisa was going out with a professional gambler named Joe Shapiro, who was a lot older (she was only twenty-two at the time and Joe was in his fifties), but very good-looking. Rose knew Joe in Chicago. Joe and I liked each other, and he always was kidding me about my accent, which was funny to him. I felt the same way: most of the time I couldn't understand a damn word he was saying. Joe came into the store a lot, often with other Chicago pals like Herbie Blitzstein and Lefty Rosenthal, both of whom, I would later learn, were "connected." They were involved with the Stardust Casino, which became a new hangout for those of us in the shop. A lot of these guys ate with us across the street at "Marie Callender's" or just a few blocks north at "Chicago Joe's."

Well, Joe and Rose would always go in the back to talk. She would say, "Franny, watch the front, and don't tell anyone we're here. If you see Lisa coming in let us know." One day, while Lisa was in the back conference room with four salesmen from New York who were trying to get her to put their line of clothing in the shop, the phone rang and I answered it. It was Lisa's boyfriend Joe.

"Where's Lisa?" he asked.

"She's in the back with a bunch of guys from New York who are trying to sell her clothes for the shop."

Well, Joe must have decided that it was a perfect time to embarrass both Lisa and me.

"Go knock on the door," he said, "and tell her I have one quick question for her. Ask her if she gives good head."

Oblivious to another expression we never used in LaFollette, I went straight to do what Joe told me to do.

"Lisa, I'm sorry to interrupt, but Joe's on the phone. He said he had a quick question for you."

"Oh sure, Franny, what is it?"

"He wants to know if you give good head."

Well, Lisa turned red, got up, stormed out of the conference room and walked straight to the phone. She lit into Joe, calling him a son-of-a-bitch and everything else she could think of. I was standing right beside her and I could hear Joe laughing so loud. She slammed the phone down and called Rose over.

"Take Franny in the back, and have a talk with her!"

I had no idea what the hell was going on, so Rose and I went to the back and I told her what Joe had said. Rose said, "You said that?"

"Yeah, what did I do that was wrong?"

Rose explained the expression to me in language I couldn't misunderstand. Now I was shocked.

"Rose, does everybody know that?"

"Hell, yes! Everybody except you."

Well, it wasn't long before Joe and three of his cronies came into the shop, laughing as they walked through the store. Again I had been the brunt of a joke. That story went around town for years. But after that when I didn't understand slang talk, I would always ask Rose. She taught me a lot.

We spent many hours in that store. Rose had me writing up receipts for a thousand dollars here, and a thousand dollars there, although I never saw anybody make these sales. Once a week I drove Rose to the bank, and she was always carrying a large satchel full of $100 bills. Again, I didn't recall seeing anybody paying that much cash for anything. But I wasn't curious (I'm still not). It was none of my business, I heard my dad reminding me from the Great Beyond, so I never asked. In fact, I've never even told anyone about it until now.

I worked hard on those receipts while Rose sat around and bitched a lot, saying how she wanted to go back to Chicago. So one day she said, "Franny, you don't have to work so hard. Nobody gives a shit whether you sell anything or not." I gave her a look of total confusion.

"The store is a front," she said. More confusion on my part. I asked her what she was talking about. She explained to me how she makes those deposits in the store's bank account—large deposits that were a hundred times what we actually were making. Now how could you do that? I knew there were magicians on The Strip, but they weren't *that* good.

"We're laundering money," Rose explained in a bit of a whisper.

Finally, a slang word I understood. It was the old idea of using a legitimate business to claim dirty money as its income.

The moonshiners laundered money back home in the pool halls and anyplace else they could in order to fool the revenuers. By this time the Bureau of Internal Revenue had turned into the Internal Revenue Service, and they were watching over these Chicagoans and their money just like the old revenuers. (It was later explained to me that Herbie was an expert at selling stolen goods, a practice known as "fencing.") Now I understood why Rose had me write up phony receipts. I never asked whose money we were laundering, but I'm sure it had to do with the casinos down the street, including the Stardust.

"If there's anything in this place you want, take it," Rose said.

So of course I ended up with beautiful clothes, while Rose would take gowns and coats and send them to her daughter in Chicago. She said she was too old to wear this kind of shit. Now I looked at this place through different eyes. Writing fake receipts in a dress shop was not going to be a career for me, but that was just fine. I made a payday, and that gave me more freedom to hopefully get out of this marriage.

One day an Army sergeant came into the store to buy his wife a birthday present. I struck up a conversation with him and he told me how excited he was about a German Shepherd dog he was getting that afternoon, and was simultaneously getting rid of the little poodle he had now. I asked, "What do you mean get rid of it"?

"I'm going to drop it off up Mount Charleston when I leave here," he explained.

It hit me that what he meant about dropping it off at Mount Charleston was just that—dropping the little dog off up in the mountains to fend for itself.

"You know it will be eaten by coyotes," I said, barely concealing my rage.

"Yes," he said, "but I've got to get rid of her."

"Where is the dog now?" I asked.

"It's in the car," he said.

"How can you be that cruel?" I asked, my rage getting closer to the surface.

"It's just a dog," the idiot said.

I asked if I could see the doomed creature, and he agreed and went out to the car to get it. Rose was listening to all of this but said nothing. I was hoping she wouldn't get mad at me for telling him to bring a dog into the store. Well, in he came with this little grey poodle, as cute as she could be, but obviously afraid of her master. She sat right beside him and minded every word. He had trained her well.

"How old is she?" I asked.

"Two years old."

"Does she have a name?"

"Yeah, her name is Fannie."

"I can save you a trip to Mt. Charleston—I'll take her".

"It doesn't matter to me," he said coldly. "I just have to get rid of her before this afternoon."

If only that son-of-a-bitch knew what I was thinking: Somebody needs to drop him off *the face of the earth*! When he left, Rose and I both had a few choice words to say about him. I asked Rose if I could leave the store to go buy some dog food. She smiled and said "Of course," and when I returned and fed Fannie, she practically inhaled the food. Rose then asked me what I was going to do with her, knowing my landlord didn't allow pets. I told her that I'd figure something out. When I brought her home, Travis was so excited; he had never had a dog before. What I ended up doing was hiding her all day, only taking her for walks at night. I kept her permanently and she remained a big part of Travis's and my life until the end of hers.

Soon into the summer of 1977, Rose told me that the shop was closing in a month or so—something to do with the fact that Lisa had to move back to Chicago because of some family situation. But I always wondered if it had more to do with somebody with a badge getting wise to the money laundering.

I don't know what became of Joe Shapiro, but Herbie Blitztein and Lefty Rosenthal would have a tough road ahead, and become infamous after the movie *Casino* came out in 1995. Lefty was a professional gambler from guess where (Chicago), who ran the casinos at the Stardust and the Fremont, and considered himself a local celebrity. He was tall and ugly, not like the guy who would later play him in *Casino*, Robert DeNiro, who is short and handsome. Of course, the wiseguys back in Chicago only allowed the Leftys of the world to stay in business as long as they looked the other way while the boys looted the count rooms. Some of that loot was ending up in our little dress shop on East Sahara. When the FBI started cracking down in the eighties, Lefty's car blew up with him in it in Marie Callender's parking lot, right across the street from where our shop used to be. Lefty survived the blast and ended up high-tailing it to Florida, where he died a natural death in 2008. Although it is commonly believed that the Chicago Outfit had tried to kill him for bringing the heat on their Vegas operation, the rumor among the people I knew was that he was actually blown up by the Feds, who made it look like a mob hit in order to start a gang war. They did this kind of thing all the time.

Herbie wasn't as lucky as Lefty. He eventually did eight years for a variety of crimes, and when he got out he went right back into the game. He somehow pissed off another gang and found himself shot to death in 1997.

These were among the first people I met in Las Vegas. What a place!

Now that the dress shop had closed, I was back to being a housewife, and at Dan's mercy because I had no job and no money. I did get a small unemployment check—$120 per week, but it was barely enough. However, because we were now in a construction boom period in Las Vegas, Dan and Jan's husband, JR, were making really good money. But it didn't matter how much Dan made because it all went into the biker bars and casinos, or into buying a new car.

I spent a lot of time alone, never knowing when Dan would get home, cooking too many meals that got cold while waiting for him to stumble in from wherever. When he did show up, he would get cleaned up and leave again, and we would have another brawl when he finally came home in the wee hours. My mind was thinking divorce but I was afraid because I would have to make a living for both Travis and me. I knew Dan would never help me with child support, but still I was tired of getting the raw end of the deal.

The speed with which I fell in love with my new dog was the complete opposite of what I was feeling for Dan. My relationship with Travis's father was like being caught in a revolving door with a wildcat—horrendous fights followed by break-ups and make-ups. When Dan wasn't talking his way back into my life, I was doing it to him. It was insanity. My excuse was that I wanted a family for our son.

Jan and JR were having problems too because of his jealousy. I can almost understand it because Jan was so striking that men were constantly after her. We talked a lot about how dissatisfied we were; we wanted our freedom. This was no way to live, watching these two men live the good life while making our lives miserable. Like me, Jan spent a lot of time alone because JR liked to drink and hang out in topless bars. He was violent with her when he was drunk, and JR was a big man and she was a small person like me, but without my attitude—I would fall out and fight 'til the death. I was so afraid that he would hurt her permanently. One night in her kitchen we made a pact to file for divorces at the first opportunity.

The beginning of the end came late one night when Jan came to my house, furious because she couldn't find JR. She had called some of his watering holes to no avail. I said that maybe Dan and JR are together. I was used to being alone all the time, but seeing Jan being treated like that put me over the edge. "Let's take a ride to see if we can find them," I said. I had my neighbor friend stay with Travis, who was already asleep—I didn't think I would be gone very long.

We cruised bar after bar on Industrial Road, and sure enough we saw JR's brand new truck parked in a bar lot right beside a phone booth, not far from Dan's car. Jan said, "I'm going to call first and see what they say and if he'll come to the phone." She went into the booth and a woman bartender answered the phone. She said she knew JR but hadn't seen him today. Jan returned to the car and, starting to cry, told me about this lying bartender. It hurt me to see her so upset. Now I'm furious.

We decided to go in and catch them all in a lie, and I was mad enough to hurt anybody that got in my way. We threw that door open and it was as if the devil himself had walked into that place. Jan went straight to JR and confronted him, while Dan took off past me and ran out of the bar—he knew he would have a fight on his hands. So I went behind the bar, grabbed this lying bartender and put her nose up against mine.

"You lied to the wrong person, bitch!"

She tried to get to the phone but I didn't let her. I then showed her what a real LaFollette "scrappin'" was—I was used to it because I had done it my whole life. I shoved her out of my way before knocking all the booze off of the shelves behind the bar. I threw bottles of whiskey against the wall and floor, breaking everything I could, as patrons raced for the exits. Not even the men dared try to stop us. When Jan finished screaming at JR, she started breaking things too, and when we were finished there wasn't one bottle of booze left in that place; a direct-hit tornado couldn't have destroyed more bottles than we did.

The bartender ran into another room that had a pool table in it, but, too bad for her, there was no exit door. I went after her while Jan finished breaking up the bar. I grabbed this bartender, pinned her arms behind her, took her back to where my sister was, and told Jan, "Go ahead, beat this bitch for lying to you." I can't remember if she hit her or not, but I had already mopped up the floor with her. I do remember one of us yanking her jeweled watch off her arm, throwing it in the floor and stomping it into a million pieces.

By now both husbands had run off—they probably didn't want to be around when the police showed up. Before leaving, I yelled back to the terrified bartender: "This will teach you not to lie. The next time a wife calls and asks if her husband is here, YOU BETTER TELL THE TRUTH!"

We left the place in ruins and started walking down Industrial, looking for our two cheating husbands. We were going to finish the job. They were so stupid and predictable, going straight to another bar up the street, probably to try to figure out whether to go home or not. Before we could get to the door and destroy another bar, a police car pulled up beside us and put us in his patrol car. We told him exactly what had happened, and, instead of cuffing us, he said, "You two don't look like the kind of girls that would like being in our kind of jails. I'm going to drive you down the road and let you out if you promise me to go home and not break up any more bars." Of course we promised and were very thankful to the officer. We were also amazed at how lucky we were. I suppose when two cute girls turn up their Tennessee accents anything can happen, and we milked it for all it was worth.

We made it home, and Dan eventually came in around five o'clock the next day—he knew I needed time to cool off. But I was actually under control now, having already blown off so much steam. Still, I told him he had to leave and that I was filing for divorce. "I've already packed your clothes." He begged me, but I didn't back down. He said, "Go back to Atlanta with me. Can't you see what this place is doing to us?"

"It's not this place," I said. "You weren't good to me before I came here. You're going to push me into going to prison if I don't get away from you. If it wasn't for Travis and how much he loves you I would have left your sorry ass long ago."

Dan left, but his begging went on for a week. In the meantime a song came on the radio that really hit home. The name of the song was "Say You'll Stay Until Tomorrow," by Tom Jones. I listened to this over and over (having no way of knowing that Jones would end up being a good friend of mine in the near future.) Well, Dan finally left and drove back to Georgia, and I took Travis and my little dog Fannie (and the wedding washboard, of course) and moved in with my sister.

Now I was living with Jan near Boulder Highway, on the east side of Las Vegas, and getting several phone calls a week from Dan in Atlanta, begging and pleading with me to come to live with him. I had already filed for divorce, but I couldn't bring myself to tell him. When the divorce became final, I started going out on the town, meeting people and loving my freedom. But Dan's calls kept coming almost every day. He still didn't know.

I had a weak moment and agreed to pack up Travis and fly to Atlanta, my first flight ever, in order to break the divorce news to Dan in person. Fannie stayed with Jan until I returned. It was there and then that I told him we weren't married anymore. He was heartbroken and desperate. He thought he could talk me into staying in his small house, but my heart yearned for my freedom (the first in my life) and Las Vegas. But I stayed in Atlanta for almost two weeks, while Dan practically smothered me.

He would not leave me alone at all: he would go to work, from where he called me several times a day. I didn't have a car, and, not being close enough to walk to anything, I was stuck. I started thinking, "How are Travis and I going to get out of here?" I knew he would never let me go or help me to get back to Vegas. I called my sister and told her the situation.

"I can get you a ticket," Jan said, "but how are you going to get to the airport?

"I don't know. I'm isolated from everything and everybody. He's watching me to make sure I don't leave. He won't even let me drive the car to the store."

"I'll go and get two prepaid tickets sent to the Atlanta airport," Jan said. "When you figure out how to get to the airport call me."

When Dan got in I told him that I couldn't take it anymore and I needed to get out and see people. "You can't keep me like a prisoner." I didn't want a full-on fight with him because I knew it would only make things worse. The next day I had a phone call from the wife of the man Dan worked for. She asked me to go to lunch and, of course I said yes; I hoped I could get her to drive me to the airport with Travis. She came by and picked me up. I'm sure Dan set it all up as a way of getting a girl friend to talk me into staying. She was a very nice lady, asking questions about how the relationship with Dan was going. I was so desperate that I broke down and told her my situation, begging her for a ride to Hartsfield Airport.

"I don't want to get involved," she told me. I was shattered. She dropped me back home and I begged her, "Please don't tell Dan anything we've talked about." She agreed not to, and so now I was back to square one, wondering what I could do. That afternoon I was surprised to get a call from this same lady who had taken me to lunch. I was even more surprised by what she said.

"If I help you get to the airport, will you promise me, you will never tell?"

Of course I promised, and until now I have never told anyone. We planned it so that when Dan was asleep in bed I would call her. When that happened I called her and watched for her car. When I saw it pull up with its headlights off, I went into Travis's room, picked him up and went quietly out the door. I was very nervous because I didn't want a confrontation in front of Travis.

Off I went, and this nice lady told me that the more she thought about my situation after she dropped me off earlier, the more her heart broke for me. She had seen many marriages like that in the South, where men ruled over subservient wives. I guess she had just seen one too many.

I called my sister as soon as I got to Hartsfield, but I had a few hours to wait, expecting any minute to be caught by Dan. I knew if he showed up he couldn't get me out of there or stop my plans to leave, but I just didn't want to deal with it. I had just destroyed a bar in Las Vegas and gotten away with it; I might not be so lucky if I destroyed an airline terminal here in Atlanta.

Thankfully, Dan never showed up, and Travis and I took our second plane ride ever.

In Vegas, Travis, Fannie and I moved back in with Jan and JR, but there was nothing out there on Boulder Highway except a few little houses and a couple of old biker bars, the most memorable being The Night Crawler. Back in Atlanta, I suppose Dan was feeling lonely and having trouble finding work because pretty soon he showed up back in Sin City, and got his own place not far from Jan and I. Do I have to tell you what happened next?

I wasn't there but a week when Dan showed up very early in the morning while I was asleep. My sister let him in and told him I was sleeping, but of course he came into the bedroom, woke me up, and started on me about how bad I was for leaving him in the middle of the night in Atlanta. All the same words passed between us that had been said a million times before. Then we started to argue, which soon led to him slapping me—big mistake.

I had the vacuum cleaner lying in the bedroom floor from the day before, so I picked up the long metal end and hit him across the face with it, knocking out his two front teeth and cutting a terrible gash across his lips. By that time my sister heard the noise and she walked in just in time to see Dan, who was bleeding terribly. She told him that he needed to go and see a doctor. She walked him to the door and out he went. She came back to the bedroom, asking what had happened.

"You hurt him pretty bad," Jan said. "He's going to need stitches."

"He shouldn't have slapped me," I said. "He's lucky it wasn't worse. He needs to learn to leave me alone." I went right back to sleep.

The next day, all stitched up and swollen, Dan's begging started in again. And once again I caved in. I'll never know why I gave him one more chance. Maybe I felt bad for all the damage I had done to his face. Like I said, it was insane. Before I knew what hit me, Dan and I were in one of those silly Las Vegas chapels getting *remarried*. It was the Little Chapel of the West, where Elvis and Priscilla tied the knot. And do I have to tell you what happened to the marriage this time? Let's just put it this way: Elvis and Priscilla lasted much longer.

Not surprisingly, Dan continued to spend a lot of time in those biker bars on Industrial or Boulder, but at least he was working at various construction jobs and providing for Travis and me. One of his jobs was on Boulder Highway at an under-construction 400-hundred-room hotel/casino called the Nevada Palace. Now it was Dan's turn to stumble into a crazy world like I had done at the dress shop. And I stumbled in right behind him.

One day in the spring of 1978 I went down to the Palace to see him, but he wasn't there. In fact, nobody was around except one guy just standing in the parking lot, looking up at this gigantic place. So I pulled up beside him and asked through the car window if he knew where Dan was.

"Who are you?" he asked abruptly.

"I'm his wife," I replied.

"I thought he was divorced."

"We were, but we married again."

"Why?"

"I have a kid, and I thought it was the best thing for him."

He finally introduced himself as the owner of the place. His name was Jim Schiff.

"Do you work?" he asked.

"No, but I wished I did, it would makes things better."

"Do you want a job?"

"Sure!" I said.

"There are four hundred rooms here," he explained, "and I would like to get them ready before New Years."

"What has to be done?" I asked. He said they have to be cleaned up from all the construction work.

I parked the car next to his big Cadillac, got out, and he showed me around the place. The casino was still under construction, but the rooms were built and the pool area was done. Schiff was filling up the pool when I arrived, so he showed me where the pool equipment was and how to turn the water on and off from the inside. The actual hotel had four big penthouse suites in it, and the other rooms were big also, but what a mess! Drywall mud was caked in the bathtubs, garbage in every room, and the construction workers had left paint buckets everywhere.

"I don't have heat in it yet," he said, "but the water is hooked up. They are working on the heat and air now. It should be on soon." After the tour, Jim pulled me aside.

"Well, what do you think?"

"I think it will be beautiful when it's finished."

"I can't find anybody that wants to work," he said. He asked if I knew anyone who could help me out. I didn't know anybody besides me, I said, but he gave me a master key, his phone number, and put me to work the next day.

I went home happy to have something to do, and a way to make my own money. When my husband came home I told him about the job, and where and how I had met his boss that day. He went into a rage.

"I don't work for that son-of-a-bitch anymore," he yelled. "I quit today and I'm not going back—and you're not going around him either." He didn't want me to work, and especially not for Jim Schiff, for some reason. But since he didn't take care of me, except for the basics, I had to earn my own money. Absolutely nothing had changed from the first time I married him.

Of course, my reply was "Yes, I am, I need a job." As usual, the fight was on. We had another physical blowout before he finally stormed out.

The next morning I had my neighbor watch Travis, and, since Dan took the car with him and didn't come home, I walked to the hotel. I arrived around 6 a.m. and began the hard work. There was no hot water, and my hands were cracked and bleeding within a couple of days, but I was determined to keep my end of the bargain, even though Dan and I fought every night when I got home. Jim would come by and check on my work about every two or three days, and was impressed at how clean the rooms were. One day he told me they were delivering hundreds of mattresses and bedspreads. Again, he asked me if I knew anyone who could help out.

"I'll pay them good," he said.

"No! I don't know anybody."

So I just kept working pretty much alone from six to six

every day. I was really exhausted, but my determination was strong, and besides, I gave my word—and you're only as good as your word, the old man used to say. As we got closer to opening, Jim finally hired chambermaids and such, so my workload became a little more bearable. (Jim was paying me in cash, under the table, and I suppose he did that with all his employees because he would later pay the IRS almost $80,000 in fines.)

When I finally got all four hundred rooms cleaned, Jim came by and helped me with the bedspreads, soap, and all the stuff that goes into a room. About two days before I finished setting up the rooms, Jim showed up with more questions.

"How would you like a front desk position?"

"I don't know anything about that kind of job," I answered, this time honestly (I learned my lesson with that hernia question back in Detroit.)

"I sent a young man to Phoenix to learn about this new electronic cash register they have," he said. "It automatically keeps up with auditing and revenue. He will train you." With this new cash register, Jim was actually talking about one of the very first computers. Jim said that because he had franchised with Best Western, he could get his gaming license, train his employees on the computer at their headquarters, and then he'd drop the franchise.

I said "Yes," and was very excited to say goodbye to that grunt work. Two days before New Years Eve that big computer arrived—it must have been heavy because it took two big guys to carry it into the lobby and set it up. It looked like it had a million buttons on it, but I was going to be trained so I wasn't worried about it.

Come New Year's Eve morning, I was there at six a.m., all dressed up and really excited about my new front desk job.

Everything was ready to go—four hundred rooms, clean and beautiful. Soon, Dave, the young man Jim had hired and sent to Phoenix for training, showed up to explain the computer to me. He showed me how to use it to rent a room, run credit cards, how much to charge for a room and a suite, et cetera. Meanwhile, I was getting nervous because the entire time not one soul walked in to rent a room. I was beginning to wonder if it was the dress shop laundering deal all over again! Meanwhile, I had to learn as much about this complicated machine as I could in just three hours, because that's how long Dave was there before he decided to go get something to eat.

"Will you be okay until I get back?" he asked

"Yes, go ahead, besides nobody has even walked through the door."

Well, Dave left and I have never seen him since. I wasn't alarmed then, but when four or five hours went by, I started thinking, "What the hell? I'm out here in the middle of nowhere with four hundred rooms and nobody to help me out with this contraption." Jim called and I told him his guy went to get something to eat; I didn't want to piss him off because that wasn't a pretty sight, and I didn't want to get this young guy in trouble. Right after I hung up with Jim, the phone rang again. It was the Las Vegas Convention Center.

"Do you people have any of your rooms available yet?" they asked.

"Yes, four hundred of them," I answered.

"You've got to be kidding," the girl on the other end said. "We have a lot of overflow because the big hotels are always overbooked on the holidays. Plus we still have dumb-asses showing up in this town on New Years with no reservation."

I told her that anybody who wants a room from me had better have a car because there's nothing for them to do down here. "You might want to let them know that before they go so far off the Strip." Well, the Convention Center gave people our number and the phone started ringing off the hook; this was the beginning of a long business relationship I would have with the Center. I gave people directions and warned them that our restaurant and casino weren't open yet.

Well, when the first guests showed up I was still staring at that huge computer trying to figure out how to start it up—Dave forgot that little detail before he left "to get something to eat." I remembered him telling me before he disappeared that our room rate was $29.68 a day, so I decided to charge thirty-dollars even, so I wouldn't have to deal with change or the machine. I also took credit cards, which I knew how to run. Back then when someone gave you a credit card you had to call the credit card company and make sure it was good.

Once I got busy, the day went by really fast, and by six o'clock, working out of a cardboard box full of cash, I had every room rented. I ended up being there all damn day until Jim walked into the lobby with a stunned, but happy, look on his face.

"Where did all these cars come from?"

I told him that I had been working with the Convention Center.

"How many rooms do you have rented?"

"All of them," I said. "Here's the money." I gave the overflowing box to him.

Now Jim was really in shock.

"How much longer are you staying here?" he asked.

"I can't leave," I said. "Someone has to keep the lobby

open. Your guy never came back!"

"What? You've been here all day by yourself?"

"Yes, and I'm really tired. My shift starts at six in the morning. I need to go home."

Jim was fuming mad at this guy.

"I spent money training this son-of-a-bitch and this is what he does? I don't want him back on the property anymore! If he shows up tomorrow, you tell him he's fired! Go home, Franny, and get some rest."

Before I left, Jim added: "I'm going to send *you* to Arizona to learn how to work this machine."

Wow! My first business trip, and plus I get to ride a plane again. Well, soon I went to Phoenix and learned all about the computer machine and trained on the Best Western franchise system—but I soon learned that Jim made his own rules.

I was now able to run that place with my eyes closed. I kept a ledger that detailed the money we made and what went out in expenses. I loved it and caught on real fast. Eventually, Jim hired a staff to help me out, so things got better almost overnight.

But the situation at home was still awful because of Dan's jealousy and the fact that I was working for somebody that he hated. Well, this one day he didn't pick me up from work, so I started walking home, arriving to find a little red car sitting in my driveway next to our car. Now I'm mad because I just had to walk home after working all day while there's two cars right here. I looked inside the red car and saw women's clothes in the back seat. Then I tried to go into my house, but the door was locked. I beat on the door and when I threatened to break out the windows, Dan finally cracked the door a little bit. I pushed it open and got inside the living room.

"Whose car is that in the driveway?" I asked.

He just stared at me as quiet as a church mouse. All of a sudden a girl walks out of my bedroom, and of course now I'm furious.

"Who the Hell are you and what are you doing in my house?"

"George said I could come over," she answered.

"Who the Hell is George?" She timidly pointed to Dan. Obviously this was some gutter slut he picked up at a bar and had enough nerve to bring into my house. I'M GOING TO KILL HIM AND HER!

Dan kept his shotgun hanging on the wall over the couch and I jumped up on the couch and pulled it down. We wrestled over that gun for a long time, until he finally overtook me. He ran with the gun, jumped in that little red car and left. He didn't even wait to take his bitch with him. I can't begin to describe how I felt, but I tore into this girl with a rage I had never known I was capable of. I gave her a few punches to the face, dragged her outside by her hair and once I had her down, I never let her up—just like the old man taught me. Since I was doing all this with a pair of high heels on, it occurred to me how to make her pay for all the pain I had been feeling inside for years. Just her bad timing, I guess. I then proceeded to give her what I refer to as "a high heel hysterectomy," if you get my drift. When I was finished, she was bleeding pretty badly, but she had stopped screaming. I think she was in shock.

I don't know where my neighbor Donna came from, but all at once she was there, afraid, and begging me to stop.

"Come on, Franny, the cops are coming," she begged.

She ran into the house and called an ambulance, then returned and frantically tried to pull me off of this woman.

Donna finally got me into her car and we took off, but not before I grabbed the woman's purse and went through it to find out who this wench was and where she lived—I wasn't through with her yet. Donna was driving fast and telling me how Dan had stopped by her house and told her to come and get this girl out of there before I killed her. But Donna told me, "Hell with her, I'm worried about getting *you* out of here." She parked where we could see the ambulance drive off with her, then Donna asked what had happened. I told her the story.

"Is he crazy?" she asked. "He knows you well enough to know better than this. What are you going to do?"

"I'm divorcing him forever. I'm through. If I don't, he could push me over the edge again, and Travis needs me. But he doesn't need this."

I went home with Donna that night—I was afraid to go home, knowing the cops would be waiting there for me. And I was not going to jail for something that I believed was justified. I went to work the next day a bit frazzled, having not slept all night. When Jim showed he picked up on it because he asked what was wrong. I broke down in tears and told him the whole story. He listened intently.

"Do you want a divorce?"

"Yes, if I don't get one I'll end up in prison, and my kid needs me."

Jim walked straight over to the phone. I don't know who he called, but I heard his part of the conversation: "Get some divorce papers ready and bring them out to my place on Boulder Highway." He gave them Dan and my names. Before noon a guy showed up with divorce papers (my second set with Dan), and I signed them. He asked if I knew where Dan was because he had to serve him also. I told him where I thought he might be: The Night Crawler. Sure enough, they found him there and served him the papers—all of this before noon! Of course, Dan called me at work and started that old pleading shit, but this time I wouldn't hear of it. This divorce was for now and for forever. Our second marriage had lasted all of four months.

Jim and I became great friends after that—but we wouldn't have if I weren't so good at keeping my mouth shut. One night after work, we were closing down the office and Jim started talking about the business and how hard it was to keep track of all his operations—he said he owned five or six big bars on Industrial Boulevard.

"Yeah, Franny, I'm sure you at least heard about one of them because it got sort of famous last year when two young girls came in and destroyed it because their husbands were there with other women. You must have heard about that?"

"It sounds vaguely familiar," I lied.

"They never found those two bitches," he said, telling me something I already knew. "But if they do they're looking at a couple of years in the slammer and about $20,000 in damages."

Not long after our little rampage, both Jan and I finalized our divorces (my second, her first.) And I was right about Dan— no child support ever arrived. In fact, he did just the opposite, he took the thing that was most precious to me: Travis. Despite the fact that I had won sole custody, it seemed that Dan wanted to make Travis his alone, and this final jab at my heart went down in the most terrifying way imaginable.

I was still working every day at the Palace, where Dan tried calling me as always, but I refused to answer. One day, I went to pick Travis up from the babysitter and I was told to my shock that his dad had already stopped by to get him. Now Dan loved Travis and I knew he would not let anything happen to him, but I was still gripped with fear at the idea of losing my baby. Obviously, the next time Dan called I answered, and it turned out that his taking of the most precious thing in the world to me was his futile attempt to get me to cave in and go back with him. He had been shocked, he said, at how fast I obtained that second divorce, and I knew that he was desperate, but I didn't think he would leave and take my child with him. He was playing a game with my life and Travis's life. Now I was feeling hatred for him!

Dan refused to tell me where he and Travis were holed up unless I agreed to move back with them, something I couldn't do again. I waited and prayed that he would give up his blackmail and bring Travis back. The authorities told me there was nothing they could do; this was long before the "Amber Alert" system, and families were expected to settle these things themselves. I called everyone in his family, and of course they all lied, saying they had not seen them or heard from them. I called my mother in LaFollette and told her to be on the lookout for them—I needed to know that Travis was safe. Mom helped me get through this, always trying to calm me by saying, "He'll give him back when he realizes that he can't use him anymore to get to you. You have to be strong."

But the days drifted into weeks, and although I was very busy at work, my heart was empty and broken and my mind was running wild with all kinds of thoughts. The weeks turned into months. Dan called every couple of months to see if I had changed my mind. He always called me at work, and sometimes he let me talk to Travis, but he wouldn't let him answer any questions, especially about where they were. All during this time, I had many offers from "well-connected" people who told me that they could find Travis and bring him back, but I didn't want Travis exposed to any violence. He did love his dad, and no matter how I felt about him, I didn't have the right to take his father from him in such a permanent fashion.

On at least three occasions Dan found a way to twist the knife a little more by promising me that Travis would be arriving at Vegas's McCarran Airport at such and such a time, on such and such a flight. I always went to the airport, where I sat for hours, but he never appeared at the gate. The fourth time Dan told me that Travis would be arriving, I toyed with the idea of not going to the airport—it was just too painful every time that last person exited the jetway and it wasn't Travis. But I decided that I just couldn't take the chance, so of course I went. It was on this day that I almost didn't go—towards the end of August—that my little boy came walking off that plane holding the hand of a stewardess. When he appeared at the gate I was standing right by the ropeline, and I cannot tell you what I felt when he came running into my arms. I picked him up and twirled around and around for what seemed like minutes; I didn't want to put him down. He held on to me so tight and kept rubbing my hair. I knew what he was feeling because I felt the same way. I just could not get enough of that little face.

We went to lunch and I was careful not to say anything bad about Dan, because he would always be his father. Travis told me how he moved around a lot, bouncing between his different aunts, some of who were mean, to the point of beating him. Now my blood was boiling again, but I didn't say what I was thinking. I told him that he will always stay with me because his dad had to work—it's easy to divert a five-year-old's mind. I only wanted him to feel happy and safe. That much I accomplished, and we have never been out of contact for even a day ever since.

After that I never had any more trouble with Dan; my dear mother was right once again. It quickly occurred to me why he had finally given Travis up: he was now five years old and it was time to put him in pre-school. I'm sure that Dan just didn't want to be bothered. Now I had just one week to buy him clothes (since Dan didn't bother to send any), but I didn't care—I was just so happy to have him back. As for Travis, he was excited to now have his own room (TV included), and I bought him new toys and clothes every week, so it was always like Christmas for him. The first few weeks I slept with him in his room until he felt secure. Now, finally, we could settle into a life together.

Chapter Three

"The Big Guy"

IT WAS HARD TO BELIEVE that just four years had gone by since I had arrived in Sin City. So much had happened, and I was meeting more people here in one day than I met in Tennessee in a year. But things were finally settling in to a routine—if only temporarily.

While Travis was gone, I had buried myself in my work, a timeless treatment to try to trick oneself out of a depression. My sister Jan always had a supporting shoulder, and to this day we are still the tightest sisters I have ever seen; we're each other's best friends. In fact, I remained extremely close to all my siblings. When my brother Aubrey saw his life come crashing down in Detroit, he came out to Vegas for a while to live with Jan and me. With this support system, I was able to pursue my new career, while having plenty of help with babysitting my newly returned five-year-old.

With the Las Vegas boom in full swing and the high-rollers arriving by plane, train, and automobile, I made it a point to learn everything I could about my new career as a hotel executive. Apparently I was successful, because it wasn't long before Jim Schiff gave me total responsibility for all the Nevada Palace's day-to-day operations, including hiring and firing employees. The casino portion was still under construction and there were always problems, so I wasn't surprised when Jim was upset about something or other. He was all business and he always seemed under pressure. Keep in mind that although Jim was civil to me, he was never talkative, or even remotely sociable, usually speaking to me only once a day, when I would tell him how much money I had deposited the night before—his chief concern

Jim sensed that I could solve most all of the problems without having to call him. My biggest concern was trying to find a head housekeeper that was any good, and I was strict about the way the rooms must look. I insisted that the head housekeeper meet with me every day because, like Jim I suppose, I didn't want to hear from all the maids about what was needed. It was the same with the construction crew, electricians, carpenters, etc.—I only wanted to talk to the head person from each department.

One morning Jim showed up in a particularly bad mood and started venting.

"This is how it's going to be from now on," he bellowed. "I want you to call everyone together, including the construction crew—all the employees. You are to tell them that if they have a problem to tell you. Don't call my office. And when I drive up here, the first staffer that speaks to me is fired!"

Wow! Of course I called everyone in and passed on the new marching orders. I wasn't proud of it but that was Jim's wish. He felt that this way he would only have one person to talk to (me), and he trusted me enough to know that I could handle most issues before they ever got to him. I solved as many as I could, but it wasn't always easy. On one memorable occasion I had gone through about ten head housekeepers before I finally found one that knew the business. After all that work to find her, her career at the Palace was very short. I remember Jim coming in to complain about her, and I guessed why.

"Who was that woman?" he barked.

"That's my new head house keeper," I answered.

"Fire her!" he said.

"What happened?"

"These people were told not to speak to me when I pull up here, and she did," he explained. I didn't argue about it, but when he left I called her in and I asked what she had said.

"I said 'Good morning, Mr. Schiff,' " the nervous woman replied.

"Do you remember me telling you not to ever speak to him?" I asked.

"Yes," she said, "but I only said 'good morning.' "

"Well, that has cost your job," I informed her. "I'm sorry, I know it's ridiculous, but he told me to fire you."

She cried, and I felt terrible, but we were back to the golden rule that the old man taught me: "The man with the gold makes the rules." It is certainly the way Vegas works.

Las Vegas was undergoing a lot of change in those days. In addition to the increasing sales of hotels to big corporations (although the wiseguys kept control of the casinos), the service unions were muscling their way into town. The fights between the pro-union and anti-union forces were downright ugly, with hotel managers such as myself often caught in the middle. The unions weren't going to succeed without a major fight with the anti-union hotels, restaurants, cab companies, etc. These businesses didn't want union workers because they would lose control of their employees, meaning that they could not fire people unless such-and-such a union thought they had a good reason.

Having seen first-hand how hard it was for an owner to succeed in this town, I was against the unions. The fact was that me and my fellow hotel manager friends always gave our employees a second chance unless we caught them stealing (and I did a few times). But once they had blown that second chance I had no problem telling them, "You're fired, now get the hell out of here!" I certainly didn't want to have to beg any union for permission to fire a lazy chambermaid or a thief on my staff. In addition, the unions were fighting amongst themselves because the Chicago mob controlled some of them and wanted the rest.

This war had started in earnest in the mid-seventies, not long after I had arrived in town, and had gotten only more violent as the years went on. By now, bombs were going off in hotels, cars, and some of our favorite restaurants, like David's Place on West Charleston Boulevard, one of the first places I went for coffee after I arrived in town.

Once or twice when I was at David's, I met a local union leader named Al Bramlet, the president of the Culinary Union, who was trying to unionize the restaurant. He had succeeded in cutting some deals with hotels, but he was known to make "sweetheart" deals with businesses that he also owned a piece of. That made a lot of people mad. Within a few months, a bomb went off in David's Place, and a few months after that, Bramlet was shot six times, including once in each ear, before he took his own desert "dirt nap." It was common knowledge that dirt naps out in the desert were on the rise, perhaps once

Al Bramlet

or twice a month. The guy arrested for the Bramlet rubout later said that Chicago's mob "Godfather," Tony Accardo, had ordered the hit. Now it seemed like the whole town was erupting, and eventually the violence hit too close to home. At the Palace, which was non-union, I had my car tires slashed one night, and the rest of the car egged on numerous occasions. Compared to Bramlet, I suppose I was lucky, but these were scary times, nonetheless.

At the same time as the union wars raged, the out-of-town corporations were imploding the old hotels, building bigger ones, and putting bean counters and Yuppies in charge. The wiseguys—the owners of the hotels that were razed—were either dying, going to prison, or just getting the hell out Dodge. We locals could all see that the times they were a'changin'.

Despite all this upheaval, my career was thriving. Jim was so impressed with my ability to make friends that he came to the realization that I should take on a new position as Public Relations Director for the Palace. It was a great promotion that not only got me out of the office, but allowed me to call my own hours and use my intuition about how to get "bodies" into the hotel. From what I could tell, I was the only thirty year-old female PR director of a Vegas hotel. I had come a long way from playing in that sinkhole in LaFollette, that's for sure.

Word of my hustling for the Palace got around, and I was shocked one day when a guest came to my office with a copy of the *Las Vegas Sun* in her hands. She pointed to a column that talked about me! It read in part:

*Fran Comer is a powerhouse lady with a
whale of a future in the business...Fran is a
definite asset to our business, and there's no
doubt that the Nevada Palace, with its huge
casino and great looking rooms, is going to set
the world on fire.*

It was the first time my name was in a newspaper, and I
was both embarrassed and proud at the same time.

I was meeting a lot of my fellow hotel professionals during
this time, having joined the various hotel associations, sales
directors associations, and convention center associations.
Additionally, every month someone in my position would host a
party at their hotel to discuss upcoming conventions, and I
attended every such get-together. It was important to know my
colleagues from other hotels, and we often did favors for one
another. My peers were big-time partiers, but they knew the
business and made this town what it was. It was at one of these
bashes that I had the first of my many adventures with Sin City
celebrities, a segment of humanity that I had zero interest in—
outside of Lash LaRue, of course.

When it was Caesar's Palace's month to host our meeting,
we all emptied out into the lounge after our business was
concluded. Lounges were very popular in those days, and most of
them featured first-class entertainment. On this night I was seated
at a little round table with a group of people drinking, laughing,
and telling jokes, when someone tapped me on the shoulder from
behind and said, "Do you really have a dog named Fannie?" I
turned around and saw the face of the singer whose song I had
listened to repeatedly after my first breakup with Dan, Welsh-

born superstar Tom Jones, who was Caesar's headliner that week.

I have to admit to being a bit star-struck, but I didn't let myself act too impressed as we bunched some tables together and introduced ourselves. Then the fun began. Tom liked his whiskey and cigars—this was before you had to ask if you could smoke. He joined in the joke telling, and he had a lot of good ones. This little party went on until sometime in the wee hours of the morning, and when I got up to leave he asked me for my phone number. And of course I gave it to him.

I couldn't wait to get home to tell my sister Jan who I had just met. I couldn't believe this was happening. Well, the next morning Tom called and invited me to his show that night. After accepting, I was told that my name would be at the door, which it was. My booth was front and center, and the show was spectacular. I got a charge out of watching all of these women (whom I later found out were on the payroll) throwing their underwear and keys up on the stage, but I just sat quietly watching the performance.

Just before the show ended, a man came to my booth and said, "Tom wants to know if you would like to join him backstage for a drink?" I did. When he took me to Tom's dressing room there were others also waiting for the singer, but when Tom came through the door he came straight over to me first, kissed me on the cheek, and thanked me for coming to the show. He introduced me around, and when the jokes and fun began Tom was very attentive, making me feel comfortable being there. I met all of his band members and backup singers, and they were all nice people. Even though my heart was pounding, I continued to play it cool.

We went up to his suite afterwards, where we talked a lot and really got to know each other. Come to find out, he was from a coal mining town also. The English and the Southerners had a lot in common. Tom told me that was because it was the English that first came and settled America. Tom's countrymen referred to sheets as "bed clothing," just like my mother had always done. People here in Vegas thought it meant pajamas. Speaking of sheets, yes, Tom and I ended up between them that night, and for the rest of his week in town.

Me with Travis and Tom Jones

I should mention here that I have never been a typical, romantically inclined woman. My friends say that I'm more like a guy, especially when it comes to

Travis celebrating with Tom Jones

the opposite sex. I have no problem seeing sex as a fun thing to do without the necessity of all that romantic bullshit attached. In fact, as a result of my horrible marriage experience, I was just the opposite: if I sensed that one of my flings was getting too attached I was out the door faster than you can say "women's lib." That being said, this was far from the last performance of "Me and Mr. Jones." We always got together when Tom returned to town, and little Travis took a special liking to the superstar.

I continued to bury myself in my work and began to drink more and be even less trusting of people, especially men. Thanks to my ex-husband, I was bitter on life, but Jim kept bringing his friends by the hotel trying to fix me up. But, like I said, my mind was being eaten up with hate because of Dan's actions, and the last thing I was interested in was a boyfriend.

One morning Jim called and said, "I'm going to come by with a friend of mine. I think you'll like him. He's going to have a lot of money someday." I just said, "OK," but in fact I was not the least impressed with money or fame.

Well, we all went out to dinner, and I immediately I had a feeling that my "date" was sleazy—just a feeling. Actually, the first thing I noticed was his body odor. I couldn't wait to get home to Travis. Jim called me later to see what I thought. "He thinks you're beautiful," Jim said. "I told him that you are also the most trustworthy employees I've ever had."

"Well, Jim," I said. "I think he needs to take some of that money he has and buy a bar of soap." Jim let out a very rare laugh and said, "You're too tough, Franny."

Despite what I said to Jim, his friend called me repeatedly to ask me out, but I made up excuses. This person, one Bob Stupak, indeed went on to become very successful in town. At the time he was pestering me, he was a high-stakes poker champion, winner of the World Series of Poker, and owner of the World Famous Historic Gambling Museum on Sahara, and "Bob Stupak's Vegas World." In 1996, Bob built the 1,100-foot tall Stratosphere Tower Hotel, with the highest observation deck in

Bob Stupak

the United States. The Mayor proclaimed him "Mr. Las Vegas," and I have no doubt that I could have become "Mrs. Las Vegas" if I had so desired. But fame and fortune have, for some strange reason, never been of interest to me. And neither did marriage now. I just wanted to have fun—why could nobody understand that?

More and more, I began meeting "mystery men" through Jim Schiff. One of the first was an Italian friend of Jim's named Ernie, who had lost everything in Cuba. Jim asked me to let him have one of the large penthouse suites to live in, adding that it would be a better situation for me as well because I wouldn't have to be alone at night. One of the first things Ernie said to me was: "Don't ever tell anyone I'm here." And I didn't. I didn't put his name down anywhere, I told housekeeping that no one goes in that suite unless they called me first, and I even had the lock changed so there wouldn't be any mistake. Ernie didn't have a car, but after we became good friends he showed me his real babies: a collection of valuable guns. He told me that if anyone ever caused me any problems to just let him know and he'd take care of it. Jim was right—I really did feel more secure having Ernie there.

If Ernie needed to go to the store I took him, and he always tried to pay me, but I never took anything from him. He ended up being one of my dearest friends, and he felt the same way about me. Sometimes I brought him to my house and he'd cook the most delicious meals. I think I was his only friend, and he regularly gave me gold jewelry just to show his appreciation. When he gave me his gold Italian horn, I was so touched that I cried. Eventually I showed Ernie how to run the front desk, just in case I had to go out.

Although I never asked him anything about his life, he volunteered that he once owned a big restaurant in Cuba, but when Castro took over, the Cuban government had seized both it and his bank account. I wish I could say more about who Ernie really was, but frankly, I don't know. As I said earlier, one of my odder traits is that I am not in the least curious, about anything; I never ask questions and figure that if someone wants me to know something then they'll just tell me. Otherwise, I stay out of their business and they stay out of mine. That's just the way I like it. Coupled with my other weird character trait—the fact that I could care less about money—I have always been trusted by a wide variety of people, from good guys to bad guys. In Ernie's case, he never told me which one he was, and I never asked.

One day at work I got a call from a deep-voiced man who told me that he was here on business and that I was recommended to him by our mutual friend, my boss, Jim Schiff. He said he had some important things to discuss, but not over the phone—would I meet him for dinner at Caesar's where he was staying? Well, I thought it would be OK since I'd be driving myself and meeting him at Caesar's Palace, where I knew everybody. Looking back, I know it seems odd that a young woman would accept such an invitation from a stranger, but I just assumed it must have had something to do with Jim's business at the Palace. But more importantly, I didn't know the meaning of the word "fear." I suppose my mountain upbringing had something to do with it. I was fully confident that I could whup any man who tried something fishy. I would tear into him the way I tore into that bar on Industrial Boulevard.

Thus I had my first dinner with "David" at Caesar's Palace Court, one of the most expensive, well known restaurants in Las Vegas. It was my first time there and I felt like a princess because that's how I was treated. David was an older man, maybe mid-forties, very worldly and mannered. He told the waiter to bring the best wine they had. When he asked me what I liked to eat I was nervous because I had never been in a place like this, nor had I been treated so well. I had no idea what to order. Picking up on my predicament, David asked if I liked steak or fish. I said steak, although I had only had it three or four times in my life.

"The lady will have filet mignon," David told the waiter. He ordered a shrimp cocktail, which I thought was a drink.

David knew that I was way out of my element, but he seemed even more intrigued with me than I was with him. I asked him why he was he asking me so many questions—I thought we were here on hotel business. He brushed my question aside and made a toast.

After a few glasses of wine I began to relax, and we ended up talking for hours after the restaurant emptied out. I was surprised that no one asked us to leave. Just the opposite: it seemed like the waiters were tripping over each other to make sure David was happy. When the evening finally ended—with no actual hotel business discussed—we made plans to see each other the next day. The next day I arrived at work, only to find three-dozen red roses in my office, with a card that read simply, "Thank you for a lovely evening." Being treated this way was a first for this LaFollette ruffian, and I was on Cloud Nine.

We met the next day for dinner at the Bacchanal Room, another expensive restaurant in Caesar's Palace. David had offered to send a car for me, but I turned him down; I kept my fun life and my business life separate from my home life, and I didn't want anyone to know where I lived with my child, Travis. Again, David started in with the intense interrogation. I told him that I was divorced, and how long I had known and worked for Jim

Schiff. Mysteriously, David seemed to know things about me that I had not told him. He wanted to know if I knew the local media and the other hotel managers, which I did. I left that night without knowing what this was all about. As skilled as he was at asking questions, David was just as skilled at not answering them. I had already assumed that he was an important person, and a few days later I would get proof of it.

Not long after that meeting, David came by the hotel, and I got Ernie to take over for me so we could go for a ride with this mystery man. David told me he had three people he needed to bring into town tomorrow for four days and he didn't want anyone to know they were there. He needed suites for all of them plus an adjacent meeting room. I assured him I could handle such a thing. I proceeded to block out three rooms under phony names. He then asked me to provide a specific list of things they needed for the conference room. I personally went out after work that night and obtained everything on the list. I promised David that no one would know anything about these visitors.

That morning at around 2 a.m., I picked up the party at McCarran, and it was evident that they had been told what I looked like because one walked up behind me and said, "Fran?" I turned around and saw three well-dressed men with briefcases. I took them to retrieve their luggage and away we went. I asked them if they needed anything that we could pick up on the way, but they said they were fine, so I took them straight to the hotel. I didn't ask their names, but I gave them my number and told them to call if they needed anything. Once they were all settled in, I left.

I received a call very early the next morning from David, making sure all went well. He then asked if I had recognized any of the mystery men. "No," I said. "Was I supposed to?" He laughed with that deep roaring voice.

"Well, one of them is one of the most powerful people in the country," David said, "and a close friend of the Kennedy family. He's Tip O'Neill, the Speaker of the House."

My face must have still been blank because he continued on.

"You don't watch the news?" he asked.

"No, I don't have time," I said.

"Well you should," he said with a stern voice. "It will help you in the future. Try working that into your busy schedule."

I took David's advice and I did start watching the news.

After David flew back East, I assumed that my life would finally settle into something approaching normal. I was frankly exhausted: In just a couple of years I had weathered the death of my beloved father, moved to Sin City, worked in a mob-fronted money-laundering operation, got divorced (and remarried, and re-divorced), had seen my son kidnapped, demolished a bar, practically killed a trollop in my own bed, and almost single-handedly opened a hotel. It turned out that these were just a prelude to an even more unbelievable period of my life.

Not a week had gone by since my meeting with David at Caesar's when he called me at work from New York. He had been calling me every day, but this was another business type of call. He had two more DC people coming to town, and he needed me to take care of them the same as I had done for Tip O'Neill. Thus I met Senator Ted Kennedy and Vice-President Walter Mondale for the first time. I made sure they had everything they needed and that they had the best rooms in town. For the VP, I had to work closely with his Secret Service staff.

No sooner had they departed then David was calling. I first thought he wanted to know how everything had gone with

Kennedy and Mondale, but he seemed to already know. David had another reason for calling.

"Feeling adventurous?" David asked. By now I don't need to tell you, dear reader, how silly a question that was.

"You're asking the girl who meets strange men for dinner at Caesar's if she's feeling adventurous?" I laughed. "Silly man. What's cookin'?"

He then asked me a question that I would hear from him countless times over the next few years: "Can you get away?" I told him of course. Now that I was PR director, I pretty much came and went as I pleased.

"I'm sending a car to meet you at the Palace tomorrow," he dictated. "The driver will have a round-trip plane ticket for you. Have you ever been to New York?"

Well, that's when it all started. Any "business" relationship I had begun with this mystery man was now progressing into something far more personal: a little business, a little pleasure. I was about to unknowingly fall under the spell of this smooth-talking, worldly man about whom I knew next to nothing. With my family here to watch Travis for me, and my new position as PR Director for the Palace, I was finally free to experience the world as a young person should, and "The Big Guy" was going to be my entré. Over the next few months and years I would get a crash course in politics, star power, US geography, mafia bosses, Hollywood celebrities and four-star hotels. Hold on to your hats!

Arriving at JFK Airport, I was met at luggage by a uniformed chauffeur holding up a sign that said "Fran Comer" (my married name). George, the chauffeur, was very polite as he grabbed my bag and walked me to his stretch limo for the ride into Manhattan. I was petrified when we went into a tunnel and George explained that we were literally under water. I held my breath until daylight appeared again. Thank God there were no leaks in that thing!

I know that so many country bumpkins are in awe of the skyscrapers, and I was too. But what really took my breath away was the insane amount of people all clustered in one place. They reminded me of the insect nests that I used to see in the sinkhole. I could never live like that, and I had no idea how anybody could. I would have been happy if George had just let me out on a street corner so I could stare at them all day like I used to stare into the static on that new-fangled television that our neighbors owned in LaFollette.

George brought me to the Waldorf-Astoria Hotel on Park Avenue, where he placed a call on the house phone, and in a flash David arrived in the lobby to greet me. He gave me a big hug and a quick kiss—it was unspoken, but we both understood that we were two free adults here to have some adult fun. He had told me at that first dinner only that he was a single man, and beyond that I knew nothing, or cared nothing. As mentioned, I am the least inquisitive person you've ever come across. I never even asked what David did for a living. I didn't care; I was living life one day at a time, maybe one hour at a time. It was springtime in New York and a magical time for Black Cat Marcum.

David saw to it that my suitcase was sent up to the room, and before you know it I was back in the limo with he and George. We stopped in front of Bloomingdale's, went in, and David ordered me (with a smile) to shop for clothes. To give you an idea of how crazy it went, when I saw a cashmere sweater I liked, David insisted that I buy one in all ten colors. That was just the beginning. By the time we finished I had to buy two new suitcases in order to haul it all back to the Waldorf.

Quicker than you can say credit card, we were back in the limo, and I was getting a private tour of Manhattan island. Against David's wishes, I insisted that we see Harlem, a place that I had read about. From there it was down the West Side Highway, into Greenwich Village—you name it, we saw it. The next three days were a whirlwind of Broadway shows like *The Best Little Whorehouse in Texas*, nightclubs, and meals with politicians I knew nothing about (like then-Lt. Governor Mario Cuomo), writers I knew nothing about (like Pete Hamill), and entertainers that I knew nothing about (like Nipsy Russell). David continued introducing me to everyone as "My lady, Franny," and I didn't object. My head was spinning with new names and places. One night we met with a friend of David's named Marty, who worked for the CIA (another thing I knew nothing about.) He lived in New Jersey and had helped David set up some sort of corporation.

I never asked how David knew all these people (crazy, huh?), but I was no more impressed with them than I was with the people who owned the television set down the lane in LaFollette. I have been told that I am rare for my complete lack of interest in celebrity. Perhaps that's why David chose me to be with him. Just like my work at the dress shop, I'd never ask for an autograph or a photo, or pry into their business. I was the perfect person to help them with their needs, nothing more.

We took the train from New York to Washington, where we had lunch with more of David's famous friends, like Senator Ted Kennedy and Vice-President Walter Mondale. Ted was very nice to me, talking politics and so forth. I could tell immediately that my guy was very close with the Kennedy clan—they seemed to have a long history together, but I still asked no questions.

Soon after the East Coast adventure, I was back in Vegas when David called me with another surprise out of the blue.

"I've got a great job for you," he said. "You can make some big money for a just couple of days work. You're going to work for Bob Guccione."

"What?" I responded incredulously. "David, I know who he is, and I'm not into smut magazines." (Guccione was the founder and publisher of *Penthouse Magazine*.)

"No, no. This is different," he tried to explain. "He's filming a TV show at the Aladdin Hotel Penthouse where he's

The 1979 Cadillac Diamante roadster

going to crown the *Pet of the Year*. He's giving her a new handmade $75,000 Cadillac and a ton of other gifts. He has a lot of celebrities coming in to be on the show, and your job would be to take a limo to the airport, get them picked up, make sure they're in their room, give them their scripts, and just take care of them. This way if they need something they have you to turn to. Your job is to take care of these people, and who's better at that than you? You'll make three grand in two days, and have fun while you're doing it."

Of course I took the job—three thousand dollars (about nine thousand in today's money) would buy an awful lot of food for Travis, and a lot of Alpo for Fannie. The stars were all staying at the Aladdin, and I was given room numbers, keys, scripts, and call times. The place was full of celebrities, each of whom received the package with all the necessary information, including my phone number as their contact, to answer any questions or arrange anything they needed. For example, one night a few of the stars wanted to go out to Paul Anka's great new spot, The Shark Club, so I made sure a limo picked them up and stayed at the ready for any that wanted to leave early. I rode with them to make sure they got back to their rooms safely. I remember singer Jaye P. Morgan, boxer Leon Spinks, and football player Hollywood Henderson on the dance floor all night. Leon was so tall and gawky that I never forgot the image of him trying to dance.

Anyway, the next morning I was eating breakfast with Sinatra cronies Jilly, Pat Henry, and Spider—a fun bunch of guys. I'm sure we were knocking back one of our favorite "breakfasts," mimosas, which are made of orange juice and champagne. At one point a group of men came by our table, and we began making small talk— I assumed they had been in our group at the Shark Club.

Hollywood Henderson with Travis

"Did you have fun last night?" I asked one of them, a tall black man that made me recall (through my mimosa haze) Leon Spinks from last night. He looked at me strangely, but said nothing.

"You're Leon, right?" I continued, assuming that he wouldn't have approached or table unless he had been out with us last night.

"I'm Ken Norton," he said, and then leaned over the table and got in my face. Norton, of course, was the boxing heavyweight champion who had famously broken Ali's jaw in 1973.

"You being from the South, I guess we all look alike, right?" he snarled at me.

He was really upset. Before I could let loose with my own temper, Jilly excused himself and slid out of the booth in order to talk to him.

"Come on, Ken, let's take a walk," he said. They walked away from the table, but in the meantime the other guys at the table were laughing their asses off. Jilly soon returned with a smirk on his face.

"I had to explain to him that's no way to talk to a lady, especially one that's in my presence," he said. I felt terrible but  I didn't see it as being that big of a deal. They laughed more when I said this. Finally, they explained to me that Ken Norton thinks of himself as being very good looking, and is even in movies and TV shows now. And toothless Leon Spinks is ugly as hell!

"So, Franny, you insulted him by getting them mixed up," Jilly said while laughing. Referring to Sinatra, he said: "Wait 'til I tell the boss this one!" All I could think of was that I guess I accidentally got even for Norton breaking the jaw of Muhammad Ali, a boxer Travis and I greatly admired.

Of course that story haunted me for a long time. When David called to check in, I told him the story and thought he was going to bust a gut.

"This is one of the things I love about you," he said. "I'll call Jilly and thank him. In the meantime, go over to Caesar's and get the works—nails, massage, anything you want. I've already set it up for you." He gave me the time and off I went.

David flew in later that night because Guccione was giving a huge party for all the people involved in the show, and he surprised me with a beautiful scarf dress to wear. At the bash, David and Guccione talked for a bit and then motioned me over.

"Bob, this is my lady, Franny," David said. Guccione thanked me for the job I had done.

"I know you did a great job because I had no complaints," he said. "And these people can be a pain in the ass." (I know he sure found that out later from his *Pet of the Year*: Cheryl Rixon never received her promised $75,000 Cadillac Diamante car— they gave her a Subaru instead—or most of her other prizes. She later sued Guccione and was awarded $86,000.) But I'm thinking to myself that Bob Guccione must have not heard the Ken Norton story yet.

*1979 Pet of the Year
Cheryl Rixon*

Well, it just so happened that good old Ken Norton had a boxing match that week, and of course we attended, sitting right up in the front row. I told David, "Don't make any plans for me to go to any after-parties. I wouldn't feel comfortable being in the same room with him."

In any event, David let me know how proud he was of the work I had done for his friend, Mr. Guccione. I had obviously passed some sort of a test with "The Big Guy," as I often referred to David, because he called me soon after to ask me out for my second travel adventure with him. If he was trying to do something to impress the un-impressible Franny Marcum Comer, he almost did it with this offer.

"Can you get away this weekend?" There was that silly question again.

"Any day now you'll be receiving an American Express Card from my corporation," he informed me. I assumed he wanted me to help him in his company, whatever that was.

"No, this will be in your name, and have unlimited credit," he said. "You can do what you want with it."

Had I been a typical girl, I would have fainted at the prospect of a shopping spree at Caesar's shops. But I preferred jeans and t-shirts, and the two business suits I used at the Palace.

So I just said, "I don't need it."

"I understand, but trust me, you will," he said. "For starters, you're going to need something special to wear for future trips you'll be taking."

For a moment I almost became inquisitive. Instead I just listened.

"Look, Franny, I've been looking for someone like you for a long time," David began. "Everyone who's met you these last few weeks has said how impressed they were with your personality and your ability to get the job done quickly, no questions asked. So let me ask *you* a question: do you plan on working in a Las Vegas hotel for the rest of your life?"

"Frankly, David," I answered, " I never have time to plan the rest of my life. I barely have time to plan what I'm doing an hour from now."

"Well, then it's about time someone did the planning for you. Here's what I want you to do: when the card arrives, buy something nice for Travis, then go down the Forum shops at Caesar's. My friend there, Lorraine, will be expecting you. She's going to help you pick out some nice clothes for the next trip. Oh, and dress warm. I'm going to show you Los Angeles."

Another place I had never seen.

With my new credit card in hand, Jan and I went and met Lorraine, the PR director for the Forum. She took us to the Gucci and Christian Dior shops, then Valentino and Ferragamo. I had no idea what these names meant, or who they were. I only knew that it made absolutely no sense to charge five thousand dollars for a pair of shoes. You could shoe all of Campbell County for that kind of money! But somehow these foreign guys got away with it. Jan, being a model, was more familiar with these names, so I bought more things for her than I did for myself. I bought a nice outfit for the upcoming trip, and on the way home bought Travis a new bike and Fannie a bag of meat bones from the butcher shop. It was my first credit card and I figured I had to break it in proper.

As in what would become my style, I traveled alone to LA, with chauffeurs taking me to and from the airports. At LAX, however, I was met not only by a driver, but David himself, who said he was so excited that he wanted to show me something right away. This time we were driven through streets crammed with cars, but unlike New York, there were no people walking the sidewalks. This was much better, I thought. I guess I prefer car traffic to human traffic.

After what seemed like an eternity, we finally arrived in what looked like a fairy tale neighborhood. It was Bel-Air, and I had never seen anything like it. As we drove around, David pointed out homes where celebrities lived, and I wondered if Lash

Larue, the only celebrity I gave a hoot about, had lived here.

"We're headed over to the next community," David said. "It's called Brentwood. It's where Marilyn Monroe used to live."

When we arrived on Barrington Avenue, the chauffeur came to a stop in front of nice two-story townhouse. David took out a key and I assumed I was finally going to see where he lived. The house was beautifully furnished, but showed no evidence of being a bachelor pad: no pictures of naked women, no golf clubs, tennis racquets or *Playboy* magazines on the coffee table, and no dirty dishes in the sink. But what really nailed it was when I peeked inside the "inside outhouse," the lid was down on the toilet. If I didn't know better, I would have sworn we had just entered a woman's apartment. But I still asked no questions.

"Come upstairs," David said, grabbing my hand. "I want to show you something."

As we walked into the bedroom, I had a pretty good idea what he wanted to show me—pretty much the same thing he showed me in our suite at the Waldorf. But before I could kick my shoes off he slid open a closet door and pointed to its fully stuffed interior.

"Voila! What do you think?"

Frankly, I didn't know what to think. Hanging in the closet were literally dozens of beautiful dresses, jackets, blouses and slacks. I was impressed with this woman's taste—whoever she was—but I was beginning to feel uneasy trespassing in her home. David noticed the concerned expression on my face.

"Don't worry—they're yours. I had Lorraine ship some things here after she sized you up at the Forum."

"How can I wear all these outfits in four days? I'll be changing clothes every three minutes. In Tennessee I changed clothes every three days!"

David burst out laughing.

"No, you can wear them whenever you like," he said.

OK. This guy was starting to scare me. I had finally freed myself from my obsessive ex, and now David appeared to be taking his place, only with a lot more style. We both sat on the bed and he tried to explain.

"No strings, Franny. I just enjoy your company and want to get you and Travis out of the casino world. Frankly, I also need an assistant who is as good with people as you are. What do you say?"

"I say 'How the Hell am I going to get all these things back to Las Vegas?'"

"You still don't understand," David answered. "They stay here for whenever you want to come to town, or whenever we have business here." Then he put the keys in my palm. Before we got up he turned to his briefcase, which he had tossed on the bed. He snapped it open and it was also full—of twenty-dollar bills.

"You can use this to buy whatever else you need for the place," he explained.

For once this Tennessee wildcat was totally speechless.

"Just one more thing," he said as he led me downstairs and out the side door. Sitting in the small driveway was a huge, brand-new Chevy.

"It's the other key on the keychain you're holding," David explained. I turned to my right and glimpsed a smiling chauffeur leaning against the limo and smiling approvingly.

"This is a boat on wheels!" I shrieked.

"I wanted to get you one with a big backseat so Travis can

sleep in the back. That way he can travel with you more often. I know how you two miss each other when you're separated. And God knows you've been separated way too much already."

I don't think the blood returned to my face until we were checking in at David's hotel room in the Beverly Hilton. The next day I got another tour like I had in New York. I especially liked Malibu because that's where I first saw the Pacific Ocean. Until this point, the largest body of water I had seen was the LaFollette Quarry swimming hole. In the limo, David explained that we had to tend to a couple of PR sort of things, and that he would be introducing me as his assistant.

"So, here, take some notes," he said, handing me a steno pad and pen. Over the next two days, I quietly sat in on meetings David had with United Artists film company. There was discussion over David helping coordinate a visit back east for Judy Garland's daughter, Liza Minnelli. Aha! David worked for United Artists, I concluded (wrongly.) Next we met with music producer and songwriter Gordon Mills, who managed Engelbert Humperdinck and Tom Jones, among others. I was really quiet at this meeting, pretending I had never met either star. They had no reason to know

Gordon Mills, Tom Jones, Tom's father, and David

about my week in Tom's hotel room last year. It might leave the wrong impression.

Somewhere in the middle of this new whirlwind, David told me what my responsibilities would be, just to make certain I was comfortable with everything. He said that, in addition to helping his VIPs when they came to Vegas, I would be in charge of the finances for his new corporation. That meant setting up bank accounts, making deposits when asked and joining him for more "whirlwinds" when needed. Additionally, since David was difficult to reach, I would also function as his appointments secretary, acting as liaison for those trying to reach him. He was always in some hotel or other, and I always knew how to find him. When he introduced me to his associates, he'd always say, "If you need to get in touch, Fran will know how to reach me."

In exchange, I would not only receive a large salary and a larger expense account, but I would be entering a world that would make life better for my son and I. He said he'd need my social security number to set me up in the corporation, and that was all there was to it. I signed on.

One day that spring I was surprised to get a call for David from my own home state of Tennessee. It was the fearsome Sheriff of Nashville, Lafayette "Fate" Thomas. Since elected in 1972, Fate was a legendary political kingmaker, who used his eighteen deputies to do the bidding of his favored constituents and politicians, including during get-out-the-vote drives. I wondered why he was calling my David.

"Well, you see, Miss Comer," he began, "we have this here parade coming up, and I was hoping we could persuade Mr. Tom Jones to come down to our little city and be the Grand Marshall. I understand that David handles his public relations."

I told him I'd pass the request on to David, which I did immediately. As I recall, at the time David was in Washington—again with Teddy Kennedy. But after I passed the message on, it hit me that we could do some old fashioned horse-trading with Fate. You see, at the time my beloved brother Bob was in jail in

Nashville County, serving four years for shooting into an occupied dwelling. Perhaps we could trade Bob Marcum for Tom Jones?

When I told David of my idea, he got on the phone to Tom and told him about the parade invitation. Tom apparently told David that he liked me—nothing more, thank God—and that he'd be happy to do the parade. Of course, David never told Tom that he'd be the ransom for my brother's release. Within a day or two, David and I were on a plane to Nashville and we went straight from the airport to the Sheriff's office, where we saw photos of Tom everywhere. He was really into him. Now I knew we had a chance.

After we settled into the meeting, David got to the point.

"Well, Sheriff, we spoke to TJ, and he said he'd do it."

"Yee-haa, that's great," yelled Fate.

"There's just one thing we need to work out," David added. "We need a small favor for my assistant here, Franny."

"And what's that?" asked Fate, his smile now not so exuberant.

"Seems her kid brother, Bobbie, who's also a friend of Tom's, is serving out five years in Nashville County on a trumped up weapons charge," David said. "He's already served a few weeks and we need to get him out."

Fate shot me a glance, then looked at a photo of Tom on his wall, thought for a minute, then issued his proclamation.

"I'm sure it was all a big misunderstanding. Besides, any friend of Tom's is OK by me. Tell

That's me with Sheriff Fate Thomas

you what, the day Tom shows up is the last day your friend's brother sits in the pokey. That will give me time to smooth things out. Work for you?"

David looked at me for my approval, and I smiled and nodded. We all stood up and shook hands on it. About a month later, Tom did the parade, and a benefit concert to boot. Fate was in all his glory, riding in the convertible with Tom at the parade, then introducing him at the concert.

As for my brother Bobby, here's how he remembers that day:

> It was a total surprise to me. One day I was transferred out, with no reason given, then transferred two more times that night. Finally, I was taken to a Nashville hotel, where a new set of clothes was waiting for me. It was crazy. While I was sitting in the room with a deputy, wondering what the Hell was going on, who shows up but Fate Thomas himself. He said, "Son, you're lucky that Tom Jones is such a great singer, and such a great friend of yours."
>
> Who? I had no idea what he was talking about but I wasn't about to argue with him. Next thing I knew a well-dressed guy named David came into the room and took me down to a limousine, and from there to the concert. Oh, that Tom Jones! David explained to me that he and my sis were doing PR for Tom and how they made the swap.
>
> Well, on my first day out of state prison, I had been treated to a limo ride, a front row seat at Tom's concert, and to top things off, I met David, who would become like a mentor to me. We were friends from that day on. In his office I saw photos of him behind the Oval Office desk with the President, and in a similar pose with Fidel Castro in his office. He was larger than life in every aspect, and never had to wait for anything. Over the years, I watched as people fell over themselves for him.

As for Fate, well, you might say that fate stepped in for him in 1990 when he was indicted in federal court in on fifty-four counts of abusing his power as sheriff. He pleaded guilty to theft and mail fraud, and was sentenced to five years in prison. He was released in 1994, and died in 2000.

When I returned home, I found an envelope from Nashville waiting for me. Inside was some sort of proclamation from none other than Fate Thomas. It said that, because of my "prudence, integrity, and ability," I had been commissioned an honorary Deputy Sheriff for Nashville and all of Davidson County, I assumed all because I bribed the Sheriff with Tom Jones so that my brother could be sprung from jail. Go figure.

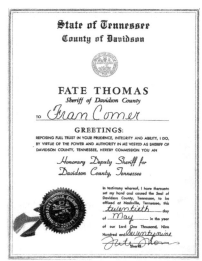

Back in Vegas, my time was now consumed with work, watching the news, spending time with David when he was in town every couple of weeks, or talking on the phone with him. As time went on we became very close and discussed everything. Being the non-inquisitive type, I never asked about his background, or how he came to be so close to those New York politicians and entertainers. I never would ask. However, I was recently told about his true background, and finally the adventures of the next few years with David all made sense. What doesn't make sense is David himself. If I had understood him, I never would have sat down for that first cocktail; I would have run like a scared Campbell County jackrabbit.

Meanwhile, the Palace was still unable to jump through all the casino-licensing hoops put up by the Nevada Gaming Control Board. It was a major setback—the spring and summer of 1979 had been spent gearing up for the casino grand opening, but the Board wasn't budging.

Jim called one morning and said, "I need to talk to you privately—today. Do you have someone to work the office for you?" Sure, I said, thinking of Ernie. When Jim showed up we went into my office, and I was nervous because this was not like him. He told me that he had leased the place out, but not to worry about my job. "Part of the lease agreement is that you keep your job and go on salary, a good one," Jim said. I was stunned when he said that I would now be getting two thousand dollars a month.

"I won't be getting your deposit slips anymore," Jim informed me, "but you still let me know your daily revenue."

"What about the casino?" I asked. That was the whole point, he said; he believed these new tenants could get approved. This way Jim would at least receive something for the beautiful casino he had built, but which had sat empty for almost a year. He proceeded to tell me that the lease payment is seventy five thousand dollars a month.

"I want you, and no else, to bring it to me," Jim ordered. "I don't want checks, I want cash. I don't care what goes on here, just make sure I get my cash every month."

"Do the new owners know this arrangement?"

"Yes, I told them this is how it's going to be," Jim replied. "They're not the owners. I will always be the owner. They don't know anything about this business, that's why they need you. I'll bring this guy by tomorrow and introduce you to him, and you can show him your ledgers." Then he left.

I made sure my books were ready, and since I worked on the books every day, that was easy. When I got home I called David and told him what went down at work, and that these people weren't going to like me because Jim had practically shoved me down their throat. They're going to think I'm a spy for Jim, which made me feel like my job was on shaky ground.

"Don't worry," he said. "Meet the new people and give me your take on them. I don't want you to worry about a job because I have a job for you if this doesn't work out."

I felt better now, knowing I had a backup. I called Ernie that night and told him what had happened, but somehow he already knew. He told me that after these guys took over he'd have to move out, because he was there as Jim's guest, not theirs. This news saddened me because Ernie had become my best friend. But, like David, Ernie reassured me that the new people couldn't run the place without me.

The next day I went to work as usual, but was very nervous about meeting this new operator. That afternoon Jim told me to call Ernie to come down and watch the front desk so that we wouldn't be disturbed in this first meeting. Jim arrived with the new lessee, Robert Mariscal, a pleasant enough man, but like Jim, not much for small talk—all business. I showed him my ledger books, including employees expenses, and my daily log from the day we opened.

The meeting went well, I thought, but I was glad when they left. The next day Mr. Mariscal called and asked me to meet him for lunch, but not to mention it to anyone. I did as he asked and at this meeting he was a lot more personable. He told me that he had an accountant coming in from out of town to take over the books, and that I should use whatever method he uses, which was fine with me since I was not a bookkeeper in the first place, and it was my least favorite part of this job anyway. Mr. Mariscal told me he had his own people coming in and he asked me to train them. Of course I was pleased to help him, but in my mind I knew he was going to ease me out after I trained these people in the business. He next asked me straight out if I was Jim's mistress, which I definitely was not. I assured him that we were only business associates, but that if he felt uncomfortable with me, I'd offer to resign. He was adamant that he wanted me to stay on, but that he wanted my loyalty as well as my discretion regarding our conversations. I assured him that I was not Jim's spy, and that all he really cared about was getting his rent on time. After the meeting I was a lot more relaxed around him and vice versa.

Mariscal brought his people in and I did as promised and acquainted them with the operation. Curiously, they didn't seem to be too interested—they were more interested in having fun being in Las Vegas, so I still spent most of my time running this hotel.

Soon Ernie and I were saying our goodbyes and he told me that he was moving to California and would call me when he gets straightened out, but I never heard from him again. I often wonder what happened to him. Jim and Mr. Mariscal finally did get the casino open when they leased it out to "Gentleman" Gene Lucas.

As a result of our hard work, the hotel really began making money. The Palace became the go-to place for all of the Strip's over-bookings; now that I knew all of the girls at the Convention Center and the key people in the other hotels, we were getting regular calls to help with the overflow guests (Vegas hotels always overbook under the assumption that there will be no-shows, but it is impossible to calculate it perfectly.) Jim complimented me on my success, and he once again felt comfortable just checking in by phone, stopping by only once a week to pick up the deposit slips, or if he needed me to take care of anybody special. One day he called to ask if I could find a position for a relative of his, an 18-year-old college girl named Laura. I was able to give her a job at the front desk, and we became so close that she ended up moving in with Travis and me. It was a great arrangement, because I now could have still another babysitter if I wanted to get out occasionally and enjoy the town or travel with David.

The only bump in the road was that I started passing out from a combination of exhaustion and hypoglycemia—the first time I even heard the term. I actually had to spend a week in Desert Springs Hospital to get my blood levels back to normal. The hospital staff was shocked when they received get-well telegrams for me from the likes of Teddy Kennedy, Tom Jones, and the Vice-President of the United States! The local news columnists again embarrassed me by telling the world I was sick and wishing me a speedy recovery. Somehow, New York columnist Liz Smith even heard about me, and

```
DES SPRNG LSV

WU LSV
02121 LGA494 1825 1-030495C113
ICS IPMNAWB WSH
10283 GOVT NFWASHINGTONDC 28 04-23 607PEDT
PMS  FRAN COMER
C/O DESERT SPRINGS HOSPITAL
2075 FLAMINGO                            (SUSPECTED DUPLICATE)
LAS VEGAS NV

DEAR FRAN:

I AM JUST DELIGHTED AT THE WONDERFUL NEWS OF YOUR
PROGRESS, AND AM SO GLAD TO HEAR YOU'RE FEELING
BETTER. WITH ALL BEST WISHES FOR YOUR CONTINUED
RECOVERY. SINCERELY

    TED KENNEDY


PLEASE DELIVER TO ADDRESSEE TODAY THANK YOU.
DES SPRNG LSV
04-25 245PPST
```

mentioned it in her column. I never even met the woman! And don't get me started on the flowers that arrived every day from David. I sent a carload of them over to the senior center.

My sister Jan was going through her divorce and dating an attorney, whom she would eventually marry. I was so happy for her, but the thought of another marriage for me was something I would not even entertain for a second. But it was wonderful to be moving on to a new life at the same time as Jan.

```
+
DES SPRNG LSV

WU INFOMASTER   1-016914C117 04/27/79
ICS IPMLGLA LSV
ZCZC 01128 (1-014051C117 1300) 04-27
TLX 684400 DES SPRNG LSV
TWX WHITE HSE WSH DLY PD
004 DLY GOVT WHITE HOUSE DC APRIL 27
MS FRAN COMER  DLR
DESERT SPRINGS HOSPITAL
2075 FLAMINGO ROAD
LAS VEGAS NV
BT

DEAR MS. COMER:
I'VE JUST LEARNED THAT YOU'VE BEEN QUITE ILL
AND ARE NOW ON YOUR WAY TO RECOVERY. JUST A NOTE
TO TELL YOU HOW GLAD I WAS TO HEAR YOU'RE IMPROVING
AND TO LET YOU KNOW YOU'RE VERY MUCH IN OUR THOUGHTS
AND PRAYERS.
BEST WISHES FOR A SPEEDY AND COMPLETE RECOVERY.
SINCERELY,
    WALTER F. MONDALE

NNNN
1411 EST
+
DES SPRNG LSV
```

Chapter Four

Rita & John and Jimmy & Rosalynn

I COULDN'T HAVE BEEN MORE RELIEVED to be beginning this new chapter of my life. My biggest goal was always to provide security and stability for little Travis, although, looking back, he probably suffered from having no dad in the house, and a mother who was always on the run. The truth is, I was working so many jobs that the poor kid didn't see me as much as he should have—I was just obsessed with making sure I could provide for him as a self-sufficient single mother without the help of a man. I know he still refers to himself as "the original latch-key kid," but my memory is pretty clear that he was always cared for and almost never left without the supervision of me, Jan, or another trusted person.

But I admit that I was also anxious to experience the world in new ways. Little could I have known that 1979-80 would be the most exciting year of my life, with one amazing adventure after another seeming to just fall into my lap. Hold on, dear reader, I apologize in advance for any whiplash you might feel.

Without hesitation, I told sister Jan about my recent adventures with David, and especially about my new condo in LA. Now we would have a place to get away and just hang out. In Vegas, David and I fell into a pattern of long phone chats every day after I got off of work at the Palace; he was always interested in what was going on in Sin City, and especially what I was doing. He regularly had me make arrangements for his political clients from back East, and everyone seemed happy with my performance.

I was now driving back and forth between Brentwood and Vegas all the time, shuttling between my PR job with the Nevada Palace and my whirlwind with David. I began taking Travis on my road trips whenever possible. When I was his age I had seen a total of four or five diners and zero hotels, but this kid was making up for what I missed. It was all five-star and stretch limos for him. He must have thought everyone traveled like this. Often he would conk out in the middle of a dinner with a prominent politician or movie star. He once told me: "I've slept in some of the best restaurants in the world."

I enrolled Travis in grade school in Brentwood but he missed his friends in Vegas, so he went to live there with my sis while I spent about two weeks a month on the road. It seems crazy, but we were all pretty happy. I could finally afford to get Travis everything he needed or wanted, while I was seeing places I never thought I'd see. I made a few new friends in LA, mostly people who also had ties to Vegas, but by and large, my best friends—like my sister, brother, and Travis—were back in Vegas most of the time.

During the winter of 1979, while burning up Interstate 15 between LA and Vegas and depositing money for Jim Schiff and David, it seemed that not a day went by that thousands of dollars didn't pass through my hands. I could have siphoned off enough to buy a new car a month, but I never took a nickel. Despite living in these capitals of excess, I still had zero interest in material things. Maybe that's why I kept receiving them: I was thirty-two years old with a great place in Vegas, a condo in Brentwood, a shiny new car, a loaded bank account and all the clothes most women would kill for, but I was happy just being single and free with Travis and Jan by my side.

If life seemed too good to be true, well, it was. David, for all the great things he was teaching me about the world, and all the security he provided Travis and I, wanted more from me than I was willing to give—but he just increased the pressure, little by little. At first it had been subtle, but it soon became more heavy-handed. Although I didn't ask, he finally told me that he was single, having been divorced many years earlier. He said he was finally ready again to commit to one person—me—and he hoped I felt the same. I cared for David, but I was in no rush to fall back into an exclusive relationship after what I had just gone through to get out of one. Besides, there were little things that registered in the back of my mind that worried me. For instance, early on David would "strongly suggest" things like what to wear to certain events, what newspapers to read, and so forth. And I happily went along with his recommendations. But the suggestions were slowly turning into commands, and I was simmering inside.

It's not that I didn't appreciate everything he was doing for me (I did), but I could feel myself being taken over by someone else's ideas and plans, and it was really beginning to eat away at me. It went against my grain to depend on anybody, and I was starting to do that with David.

But the worst part was the fact that his controlling ways were increasing all the time. Even more infuriating, he started telling me that he had our next six months all planned out—down to the day! Hell, I couldn't be bothered with planning tomorrow, let alone next year, and I was happy to be that way. I have only recently heard the word "Svengali," and, looking back, it is clear to me that David knew the word all along because he had eyed me from a distance and determined that he could mold me into anything he wanted—and he almost did. I needed to come up with a long-term plan that would get me out from under his shadow. As luck would have it, I actually came up with something.

One night my sister Jan and her boyfriend (and soon to be husband) Jerry Gillock stopped over to the apartment I shared with Travis and my brother Aubrey for some barbecue, and as the night wore on we were knocking back some beers and talking about the good old days in Campbell County. I remember the discussion turned to our grandfather's restaurant downtown.

"Sis, I just thought of that cigar store on the corner," Jan said. "Remember that?"

"Oh, sure," I said. "Daddy used to trade the owner some hootch for a box of Cubans."

"I was thinking about the time we got in trouble there," Jan recalled.

"Oh, God, yes. I almost forgot about that. I don't know how I could. My backside was sore for a week."

"Don't stop now," Jerry said. "Details!"

Jan and I looked at each other to see who would tell the story. She tipped her Budweiser to me.

"Well," I started, "the store had this gigantic wooden Indian statue out front. It was the coolest thing. I had just watched a Marx Brothers double feature at the Cherokee when mom took us into town, and I thought Groucho was the craziest thing I had ever seen. I began drawing mustaches, eyebrows, and glasses on all the pictures in my schoolbooks. I was drawing Groucho's cigar when I thought of that cigar store Indian. One day I took a can of black paint and a brush from art class. Walking through town on the way home, I told Jan my idea."

"I remember laughing until my sides hurt," Jan said. "You were such a bad influence."

"Anyway, when we got to the cigar store, we waited until no cars were driving by. Jan, you were the lookout while I painted that poor Indian up like Groucho. All of a sudden, Mr. Franklin, the owner, came running out, screaming his head off."

"I never ran so fast in my life," Jan added. "But Franklin recognized us. He was yelling, 'You Marcums are going to pay for this!' "

"Yeah, plus we spilled that paint all over ourselves," I said. "So we were pretty well convicted."

"Have you noticed they don't have any cool statues like that here?" Jan asked. "Weird, because they have everything else. What this town needs is a good statue museum."

"Yeah," I added, "but with all the famous people who perform on the Strip. That would be a hoot."

"You know, this is the entertainment capital of the world," Jan said. "And no one in this town gives them any recognition. Every entertainer I have talked to feels they haven't made it until they play Las Vegas. There should be an Entertainer's Hall of Fame, full of statues of the stars."

Of course, we were just having idle conversation, but Jerry, who was a lawyer and businessman, finally piped in.

"You know, that's not a bad idea," he said. "Not bad at all—an entertainer's hall of fame, complete with wax figures."

Well, I suppose we had drunk too much, but soon we were talking all excitedly about how we could do it. Since I knew all the hotel PR people, and Jan and Jerry knew how to run a business and handle legal matters, we all knocked bottles and agreed to get serious about it the very next day.

The plan we came up with was this: it wouldn't make financial sense to construct a building for the project, so I volunteered to use my hotel contacts to see if one of them would be interested in leasing us some space. Visitors would be charged six dollars for the museum tour, after which they would—hopefully—empty right out into the hotel's casino. Being in the business, I knew that was all any hotel wanted: "bodies" in the casino. That's how we referred to them, "bodies." When any hotel booked an entertainer it was in hopes that when their show was over, the bodies from their showrooms would empty out into the casino rooms to play the tables and machines. And if you were a good entertainer, a headliner, you could fill up a big showroom like Caesar's with 1500 bodies, or whatever maximum was allowed by the fire code. A hotel would try to get two shows a night from the entertainer, and of course, they wanted to book someone that would pull in bodies not only over twenty-one years of age (old enough to gamble), but also old enough to have money. Therefore, the target was middle-aged and over.

I remember when Caesar's booked Willie Nelson, who was a great entertainer, but for some reason his fans didn't exactly make a bee-line to the tables after his shows. He did fill up the showroom, but the executives at Caesar's told me that his fans didn't spend enough in the casino, and therefore they wouldn't be bringing him back. He attracted people, but not high -rollers (people with a lot of money to drop on the games). I wondered if it was because his fans were more interested in doing what Willie was going to do after the show: get loaded. He would always "toke up" before he went on stage and after he came off. My sister and I were there for one of those crazy nights. Yeah, we toked some weed with him, and had a few laughs together before he went out on stage.

Jan and me partying with Willie

Before I knew it, I was not only running the PR for the Palace, but also having meetings every day to get this new museum venture off the ground. I saw having my own business as a way to eventually quit the Palace and establish my independence, especially in regards to David.

As expected, David was dead-set against the idea of the wax museum. First, he tried to say that it was too risky, that it would never succeed. When that didn't work he attempted to guilt-trip me by saying that he was paying me good money to make myself available for his clients. He said he was worried that the museum would affect my ability to travel, but I assured him that Jan and our brothers agreed to fill in for me whenever he needed me to hit the road. His work would still be my priority, so there was no need to worry. But he still wasn't happy and continually put the museum idea down—of course, it was more about him possibly losing control of me if I became financially independent. His opinion had no impact on our plans, however.

Before we looked for investors or celebrities, we needed to find a location to house the museum. That turned out to be the easiest part: a good friend was the GM at the Tropicana, and he thought the idea was fantastic, so he took it to the board and they quickly OK'd our proposal. It turned out that they had a lot of newly empty space in their Atrium, so our timing was perfect.

Jerry had written a great business plan that was all accounting mumbo jumbo to me, but it certainly had impressed the board with the idea that they would turn a nice profit.

Jerry determined that the extensive renovations and the cost of molding the life-like wax figures would run into the mid six figures, but that was his and Jan's department—I would be responsible for tracking down all of the celebrities, talking them out of their clothes (so to speak), and getting them to sit down for the plaster face casting. Jan and Jerry came up with our first, and major investor, a local community pillar named Charles Vanda. Charles was a former CBS producer and director in Hollywood who had moved to Las Vegas in the sixties. He had directed or produced icons like Jimmy Stewart and Cary Grant, and great comics such as George Gobel, Milton Berle, Abbott & Costello, and Jack Benny. By the time he invested with our "Las Vegas Entertainer's Hall of Fame," as we named it, he was the Director of Concert Programing at the University of Nevada Las Vegas. Forrest Duke, a renowned columnist for the *Review-Journal* was another early booster. These men and others comprised our "selection committee," which chose the performers we would memorialize in wax.[3]

After securing the investors, we began renovating the Tropicana's Atrium. We used our brothers Bob and Aubrey to help with construction, and we would later use them as tour guides when we opened; it would be a family thing, and they were thrilled to be working on such a project. We hired former Italian actress turned award-winning sculptress, Lia Di Leo, who had a studio overlooking Sunset Strip, to execute the wax faces for the

---

[3] Other members were: Walter Kane, Leo Lewis, Jeanne Magowan, and Lenny Martin.

living, and bronze busts for the deceased honorees, while Kent Armstrong designed the pedestal displays.

Despite my workload at the Palace and the new museum, I continued taking care of any of David's VIPs that came into town that didn't want anybody to know they were there—in other words, to keep the press from knowing. And Jan went on to marry Jerry, and began helping him build his business. I don't think he took his career seriously until they married and Jan put her foot down on his drinking and partying. She helped him remodel his office, hire competent attorneys, and set up a good billing department. She spent almost every night wining and dining future clients for Jerry's firm. She really turned his life around and helped make him a very successful attorney, and everyone knew she was the wind beneath his wings. David didn't like Jerry very much; he thought Jan was too good and too smart for him. But I reminded him that it wasn't his business. If Jan was happy, that's all that counted. We will be happy for her and with her.

Jan and I now had offices at the Trop, but I was usually on the run, as far away as New York, tracking down the stars and convincing them to donate clothes and to sit still for an hour while their faces were set in plaster. This led to some strange but mostly pleasant experiences, and it was incredible how friendly they were—I don't recall one diva display from any of them. I went to Liberace's home

Liberace signing autographs with Jan and me looking on

and he was the best. He not only gave us one of his beaded suits, but also one of his priceless pianos to seat his wax figure next to!

The only remotely awkward meeting I remember was when I went backstage at the Frontier, where Roy Clark, of "Hee-Haw" fame, was the headliner. Roy, who was relaxing in the dressing room after the show with country star Tammy Wynette, was very friendly and agreed to participate in the museum, sit for the plaster cast, and give me his stage clothes. In fact, he handed me the boots he wore that night!

Well, one thing led to another, and before I knew it we were

knocking back rounds of Kentucky whiskey and getting "plastered" the old fashioned way. We were getting pretty chummy, telling jokes, et cetera, when all of a sudden I noticed Tammy shooting me looks that could kill—I quickly picked up on a jealousy thing

Liberace at the piano he donated to us just so his wax figure would have somewhere to sit

and wondered if I had intruded on some fling the two were having.

"What the fuck's her problem?" I asked Roy.

"Don't you worry about it," Roy mumbled back through the whiskey haze.

"I don't," I answered.

I never found out what was going on, but we continued partying while Tammy just stewed in the corner by herself. Very strange.

Among the first wax figures we completed were: Frank Sinatra, Dean Martin, Sammy Davis, Jr., Buddy Hackett, Tom Jones, Liberace, Roy Clark (boots and all), Jerry Lewis, Ann-Margret, Paul Anka, Tony Bennett, Shecky Greene, Wayne Newton, Debbie Reynolds, Don Rickles, Elvis Presley, Danny Thomas, Red Skelton, Shirley MacLaine (a friend of The Big Guy). Deceased icons who were cast in bronze included Louis Armstrong, Judy Garland, Louis Prima, and Nat King Cole.

The wax figure of Buddy Hackett

Over two hundred guests attended our July 8 grand opening. It was the beginning of a great success and one local columnist called the Entertainer's Hall of Fame "a top tourist attraction."

Me, Lia's ass't, Jerry, Janice, and Lia Di Leo

Once the museum was up and running I went back to spending about half of my time in Brentwood, and David now visited me there more than in Vegas. He showed up pretty regularly, and was very often taking phone calls in the middle of the night. One of his most constant phone companions was Ted's mom, Rose Kennedy. I didn't eavesdrop on their conversations, but it seemed like Rose thought of David as another son. In fact the only time I ever saw David cry was when we watched a television show about the assassination of Robert Kennedy, whom David had worked for. David's CIA pal from New Jersey called often also.

I had set up bank accounts in my name in Vegas and LA, and every couple of weeks I'd get a briefcase full of cash to deposit— always just under $9,000 into each account so the IRS wouldn't get interested. Occasionally I couriered cash to someone else, but most of the time I just took phone messages for David. Many of those messages had to do with David's celebrity clients, such as Liza, Shirley MacLaine, Tom Jones, or Engelbert Humperdinck.

I had a little reprieve from my heavy schedule when, out of the blue, the Nevada Palace closed down temporarily due to bankruptcy. It had nothing to do with the hotel operation, which I had worked so hard to make succeed; it was something on the casino side that I wasn't completely privy to. But apparently Mr. Mariscal's financing was not all that he said it was and the casino never received the operating funds it was promised—somewhere around a million dollars. That was the end of Mr. Mariscal's involvement with the Nevada Palace. We eventually reopened, but I enjoyed the breather and it gave me the time to concentrate on getting the museum off to a proper start.

I believe it was during the summer of 1979, not long after the museum opened, that David showed up at the Brentwood place early one afternoon with a friend he had just picked up at LAX.

"Franny, meet John Jenrette, the distinguished Congressman from South Carolina, and Tip O'Neill's good friend."

"Nice to meet you," I said, wondering what he was doing in my apartment. He appeared to be in his mid-forties, with a full head of dark hair, but the main thing I noticed was his breath: he had obviously gotten loaded on his flight from Washington. I asked him if he'd like something to drink. Coffee? Iced tea? Soda?

"I could use a Jack Daniels straight up, if that's possible. I had a bumpy flight," he replied.

When I returned with drinks, he and David were sitting in the living room. As I was handing out the cocktails, I caught Jenrette sizing up my ass. Women have a sixth sense about when guys are checking you out, but this lush wasn't even discreet about it. I was about to leave the men alone to their business when David stopped me.

"Franny, don't leave. The whole reason I brought John here was to talk to you."

Now I was confused again.

"John's in town for a few days and he doesn't know anybody," David said. "We were hoping you could introduce him to one of your girlfriends, so he'll have some company."

Company? I thought. I knew enough about politicians from Campbell County to know that when they said "company" they meant the kind of company you have under the sheets. Now I was willing to do a lot for David, especially after all he'd done for me, but if he was going to start having me run an escort service, I wasn't about to go there.

Before going any further I managed to get David alone in the kitchen for a minute to see what was up. He said not to worry, that he had no intention of getting me to do this again. He promised it would just be a one-time thing. Jenrette was a potential new client and David just wanted to get him a dinner date.

Although I said, "OK, let me make a call," I didn't really have my heart in it. But it was clear to me that this was an important contact for David, and I didn't want to harm his business.

I went along with it, but, just to be safe, I called my friend Dina in Santa Monica, who came from a "connected" family in Kansas City that was skimming two casinos in Las Vegas. If this congressman tried anything fancy with her, he'd end up sitting with the fossils at the bottom of the La Brea Tar Pits. I made the call and David took the horndog back to his hotel near the airport before catching his own flight out to New York. The Congressman later took a cab to Dina's place.

Well, wouldn't you know, around three a.m. I was awakened by my phone ringing, and guess who was on the other end? Congressman John. In the background I could hear things crashing and the unmistakable sound of Dina screaming.

"Franny, you've got to come get me!" John said hysterically. "This crazy bitch keeps hitting me with a broomstick. She's out of her fuckin' mind!"

Poor John, I thought. Afraid of a little girl. Hell, I'd been beating up guys twice my size since I was six years old. Now this alky from South Carolina wants a girl—me—to come rescue him. What was the world coming to?

I told him to get out and walk over to a nearby Denny's Restaurant and I'd pick him up in fifteen minutes. When I got there he looked like he'd been through a war and sounded like his battlefield canteen had been full of gin. I didn't ask what happened. I didn't care. I just wanted to get back to sleep. Since I didn't feel like driving all the way down to his hotel, I decided to take him back to my apartment. I just wanted to get him onto the sofa until the next morning. As you might imagine, I had absolutely no fear of him trying anything with me. I'd cut his balls off and throw them out onto Barrington Avenue for the squirrels to play with.

The next morning, John was apologetic, telling me that when he drinks he becomes a different person. He begged me to forgive him, and to please come to visit he and his wife the next time I was in Washington.

Wife? Whatever. I drove him to LAX, and indeed he did seem very nice sober and continued to be apologetic.

Well, a few weeks later, David took me back to DC for meetings with various high-ranking Democrats, and we made a point of calling on Mr. & Mrs. Jenrette for dinner. Rita, the congressman's wife, was a real Texas beauty, smart as a whip and a real sweetheart. Knowing what I knew about her husband's performance in Santa Monica, I quickly concluded that he didn't deserve a woman like Rita.

John and Rita Jenrette

Ironically, the two had met three years previous when she was in DC digging up dirt on Democrats just like John Jenrette. She was working for the Republican National Committee, with the title of "Director of Opposition Research." She later told me that she had been specifically asked to get dirt on John after he saw her in the Capitol Building hallway and pretended to be a tour guide just to get her to walk with him.

Rita and I started a great friendship after that, speaking on the phone quite regularly. She told me that their mutual attraction had been so intense that she quit her job with the Republicans, married John a few months later, began working for a subcommittee of world hunger under *Democrat* Hubert Humphrey, and wrote a major report on the Food for Peace program. John became the Democratic "Whip," the guy who coordinates and rounds up the votes on bills, and soon the local press described the dynamic Jenrettes as the hottest couple in DC. Rita told me all about the soon-to-be infamous incident where she (wrapped in head-to-toe mink coat) and John had sex behind a column on the outside steps of the Capitol Building. I've heard that now she says they only smooched, but that's not what she told me in one of our frequent girl talks.

Rita also confided in me that she had caught her husband with many women, but that he always managed to convince her that it was the booze, and not him. I knew she was wrong, but I didn't butt in to their private affairs. However I felt sorry for Rita, and wondered when someone like Santa Monica Dina would pop up with her broomstick—or worse—and ruin everything Rita had worked for. From their travels together, my own David came to learn that John regularly pinched the asses of airline stewardesses and often had to be carried off of planes stone-cold drunk. But Rita stood by her man. When she convinced him to enter an alcohol rehab center in her Dallas hometown, she paid him a surprise visit and caught him messing with one of the rehab nurses. But she *still* gave him another chance. I'd have taken a bat to his skull a long time ago, but that's just me. Jenrette had no idea how lucky he was to have this beautiful, forgiving, and non-violent woman in his life. In any event, I would soon be proven right about their marriage blowing up, but I was wrong about the way it would happen; it wasn't at the hands of a crazed fling with a broomstick, but a wolf dressed up in "sheik's" clothing (you'll get the joke soon.)

Rita and I chatted away, exchanging phone numbers at the end of the night. We stayed in touch for the next couple of years—more about that later. She was very intelligent and so sweet that I felt bad about setting her husband up with Santa Monica Dina. That would certainly never happen again.

Sometime that fall, I was back in Las Vegas, and during one of my daily phone chats with David he announced another whirlwind.

"I want you to see Lorraine again at the Forum," he said. "After all, you have to look nice when you meet a real VIP, Judy Garland's daughter."

Whatever. The most important VIP in the world, as far as I was concerned, was Travis, and I didn't need any special clothes to wear for him. Besides, I was more interested in just slumming it with David, Travis, my sis, or my dog Fannie than meeting the daughter of the woman who was in *The Wizard of Oz*.

For this trip I flew to DC's Dulles Airport during the second week of November 1979, and I was met there by another limo that took me to the Watergate Hotel. David was already in the suite chatting with Ms. Minnelli when I arrived. Liza was in town for a week of performances at the Kennedy Center, which is just down the street from the Watergate. She was very hot at this time, having just had a big hit singing the *Theme from New York, New York*—before Mr. Sinatra— from the Martin Scorsese movie of the same name. After we were introduced, Liza and I began going over her schedule of press interviews, dinner parties, travel to and from the Center, and a thousand other things.

Back in our suite that night, David, who was a smoker, was frantic to find an ashtray, so I fessed up that I had already stashed all eight of them into my suitcase. "I collect them from my travels," I explained. "You should see the ones I got at the Waldorf. But these are even better, they're made of pewter!"

"OK, but don't get me in any trouble," he said. "Believe it or not, I have a reputation in this town." He would soon prove that to me, and then some.

I attended a couple of performances of the sold-out review, watching from the wings with David. Also backstage was Liza's pal, the artist Andy Warhol with his boyfriend Bob. Joining us at the event were none other than David's other friends, Congressman John Jenrette and his wife Rita. Once, when Rita was distracted, John turned to me and made that zipper-across-the-lips hand motion. I smiled and gave him the thumbs up: his secret was safe with me, just like everybody's secrets were.

After the second show, we all piled into a stretch limo and were taken to a reception for Liza at the Moroccan Embassy. As we exited the limo, David pulled me aside and whispered in my ear.

"Please be Fran Comer in here, not Black Cat Marcum," he suggested.

"Whaaaa?"

"Once we step inside we're not on US soil anymore.

"What the hell?"

"I mean that if any laws are broken, we'll end up on our own in a Moroccan jail."

When I didn't say anything, he jumped in.

"I mean no ashtrays!"

"Gotcha," I agreed reluctantly.

Inside the Embassy, the Moroccans treated us with great

respect, and they were absolutely entranced with Liza. I never determined what the connection was between Liza and Morocco, but there definitely was one. Eventually we were ushered into a beautiful dining room, where we were joined at our end of the table by Liza and her fiancé, Mark, Andy Warhol and Bob, and the Jenrettes. I looked around the room and was a bit startled: for the first time I was surrounded by real foreigners! Since they were all speaking Arabic, I had no idea what was being said, but this was a time to keep my mouth shut and learn whatever I could from the experience.

Of course our end of the table being all Americans, we chatted amongst ourselves. I was on my best behavior, but I had to bite my tongue because the food was awful, and it was all could do not to go into the kitchen and show the chef how to cook meat until it's finished—mine was still bleeding on the plate! I had never seen such a thing. I think we all agreed about the meal, but no one said it aloud—we just took small bites and looked at each other. Actually, Andy Warhol and his date didn't agree; they thought the food was wonderful. But I thought to myself, "This guy is touched upstairs anyway." I could just not understand why all the hoopla about this little fella. He looked like he had just climbed out of the bed before he came here: his shirt was too small, with lint all over it, and his hair was a disaster. But I just observed and stayed sweet to everyone. When things started to wind down I whispered to David, "When we get out of here, you're taking me out for a good greasy hamburger." He laughed and whispered what I had said to the others at the table.

As for John Jenrette, he was nice enough, but really hit the "sauce," if you know what I mean. He really had a problem. I hoped someone else was driving the Jenrette's car home.

All in all, the entire evening was certainly an experience I would never forget.

One afternoon towards the end of the trip, a bellhop arrived at our suite holding a garment bag. David handed it over to me and asked me to try it on and see if it fit. It was a beautiful dress suit and silk blouse, and it did fit.

"What's this for?" I asked.

"A special meeting today, and I just wanted you to look your best," he said. "Is it alright?"

"It's great, but—"

Before I could ask another question, Liza arrived at the suite.

"I can't believe how nervous I am," she confided. "Last night I had no problem in front of two thousand people, and now I'm wreck with just one person."

"What are you talking about?" I asked.

"You don't know? In a half hour—"

Before she could finish, David cut her off.

"Let's just surprise Franny," he told her.

"Holy crap," Liza said. "I can't wait to see your face."

Liza and David waited while I went off to put on my makeup and new outfit. When we went downstairs to leave, I saw a black town car pull up with US GOV license plates. I turned around to see if some Senator was nearby waiting for a lift. Just then two dark-suited men got out of the car and walked over to David, who then asked Liza and I to show our ID's, which we did. Then we were all allowed to enter the car. The two men in front had small earplugs attached to wires, and they occasionally appeared to be speaking into their sleeves. I turned to Liza, who was biting her nails for all she was worth.

"Did we do something wrong at the Moroccans' place?" I asked David.

I had made him laugh for the umpteenth time. Liza also cracked up.

"No," he said. "Remember when I asked you for your Social Security number? That was so that these two gentlemen up front could check you out."

Oh, my God, I thought. Did these men find out about the bar I destroyed on Industrial, or the woman I gave the high-heel hysterectomy to?

"And guess what?" David continued. "You passed with flying colors. So now we're going over there to see where they work."

He pointed out the window to a building I actually recognized: the White House. What the—? We drove through the gatehouse, right up to the front door, had our ID's checked again, and were given badges to wear around our necks. David seemed to know his way around, as well as some of the people who worked here.

"Look at those ashtrays," I said in the lobby, just to freak David out.

"Don't worry," I laughed. "They'd never fit in this teeny little pocket book you made me bring."

"It's called a 'clutch,' Franny," David informed me.

"Well, it's not big enough to clutch nothing," I said. He shook his head and tried not to laugh.

He then led Liza and me down a hallway where we met a secretary who rose to greet us.

"Hello, David, great to see you again," she said with a southern accent.

"Hi, Susan, please meet Liza and Fran."

After we shook hands, Susan said, "He's all ready for you." She opened the door to the Oval Office, and there he was, President Jimmy Carter, chatting with his wife Rosalynn. OK, David, now you've impressed me, I thought. It was very obvious to both Liza and me that David knew the President on a personal basis, since he was the one who had arranged this visit to the

(L-R) Rosalynn, David, President Carter, me, unidentified woman and Liza Minnelli

White House (which incidentally created good press for Liza the next morning.) My mind was racing as I took it all in: the furnishings, the artwork, not to mention the history that had taken place here. My daddy would have been so proud to know that I was about to meet a President—and a Southern one at that.

I shook hands with President Carter and the First Lady, but mostly stood in the background while some photos were taken of the President and Liza.

We made small talk and I was very humble and gracious to the President and First Lady, telling them how honored I was to meet them and that it would be a memory I would always cherish. (Wow, what an honor for someone like me.)

Rosalynn was timid, but President Carter was so friendly and down to earth that I began speaking to him as if we had grown up together. Carter and I had both lived in Atlanta, so we had that in common. I asked him things like whether he remembered Atlanta's "Watermelon Day" celebration every August 3rd. (He did.)

Mr. Carter told David, "Please come back and bring this young lady with you, she's a delight." David said that he would— "besides she will be helping out with our re-election committee."

"Wonderful," said Mr. Carter. "I look forward to your next visit."

I had no idea what David was talking about, but I smiled and went along with it. The visit lasted all of ten minutes, which included a photo session, before we were ushered out and driven back to the hotel. I naturally assumed that this would be my only meeting with a President, and I was happy with that. But it would actually be the first of many meetings with Carter and his people—thanks to David I would meet President Carter at least three more times, including for dinners in the private residence.

The ride back gave me the opportunity to tell Liza about our new Entertainer's Hall Of Fame and to let her know she was an inductee. She was very flattered and said, "I work a lot in Vegas. I love that town." It also gave me the perfect opportunity to ask for her clothes (so to speak) so that we could dress her wax figure and invite her to the opening. I asked if she would sit for a plaster face mold, and she happily agreed, giving me the telephone number of her scheduling person so that we could set it all up. What a great lady she turned out to be, and she was so sweet and accommodating to me. I saw Liza a few more times when she came to Vegas to perform, but we never became what I would call close friends.

When we were back at the hotel, David said, "You handled that wonderfully. You really have caught on quickly how to handle people. Obviously you have a knack for it. Do you use that talent to handle me?" I laughed and said, "I learned from the best—you."

"I know, and that's what worries me," he said.

We both felt bad at having left Travis behind, and David made a vow that we would include him on our future trips whenever it was humanly possible. My boy was especially upset when he learned that I had been to New York City. I don't know what movie he watched, but somehow that little guy knew all about the skyscrapers and he was desperate to go to the top of one, especially the Empire State Building. Of course David, who really loved Travis, wanted him to have anything he desired, so as soon as he heard about Travis's dream, the plans were made—with a big surprise for both of us as icing on the cake. So off we went.

Travis at the Empire State Building

When the three of us got to New York, we headed for the Empire State Building straight away, and I don't know who was more amazed by that view from the observation deck, Travis or his hillbilly mother! However, instead of heading to a hotel after our hour in the clouds, David said, "I'm going to rent a car and were going on a little side trip."

"Where?" I asked.

"It's a surprise for Travis, he'll love it."

David didn't tell us until we arrived, but we ended up about two hours west of New York, in Deer Lake, Pennsylvania. We passed through a security gate (in the middle of nowhere), and then pulled up to a private, very secluded compound before parking in a wooded area with lots of large cabins all around. When we got into the place, three very large black guys came out to greet us, and I could tell that these people knew David, who asked them: "Where's the champ?"

"I'll take you to him," one guy said. We walked through

the woods to a cabin that had a boxing ring in it, and Travis spotted him first.

"Oh, my God, it's Muhammad Ali!" he squealed.

And sure enough, he was right. Travis and I both attended all the boxing matches at Caesar's (usually within feet from the ring), so we knew who the stars were. At one Sugar Ray Leonard fight at Caesar's, Howard Cossell, whom I knew casually, walked up to me and said, "Jesus, Franny, you're splattered," Whereupon he took out his handkerchief and wiped a streak of Sugar Ray's blood of my forehead. Sadly, my white linen jacket never fully recovered from the bloodstains.

Ali came and over gave David a hug and a handshake, and then David introduced me.

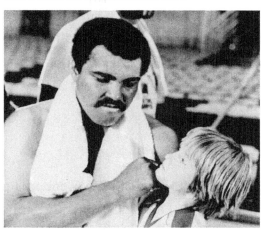
Muhammad Ali with Travis

"Muhammad, this is Fran," he said. "She's my lady."

We shook hands and Ali introduced me to his wife, Veronica Porsche, and their kids, Muhammad Jr., Hana and Laila. Travis was in heaven when the Champ messed with his hair and let him throw some punches into his stomach. Ali pretended he was hurt and stumbled backwards.

"Who does this kid think he is? Frazier?" Ali joked. "No, it can't be Frazier because Frazier doesn't hit that hard. Plus he's too pretty to be Frazier. Not as pretty as me though."

Veronica was a beautiful, well-educated woman, and her

kids were about Travis's age, so after a few more minutes with the Champ, the youngsters took off playing like they had known each other their whole lives. At some point I told the Champ how I had humiliated Ken Norton, the guy who broke his jaw. A big smile came over his face, then he hugged me and turned to one of his managers.

"This lady and her boy get the full treatment whenever I fight," he ordered. "Front row seats, limos—the works. Anybody who does that to Norton is part of the family forever!"

Soon, David, Ali, and a few of the guys went to another cabin to talk, but I wasn't invited in on this one. I didn't mind; everyone was so nice to me, and this was a beautiful place to just relax. I enjoyed walking the grounds with Veronica and seeing some actual greenery for a change—it was one of the things I missed most about LaFollette.

When David came out of his meeting with Ali's people he said that we were going to leave Travis here for a while because we have another meeting to go to. What? I can't leave my boy here with strangers!

"He'll be fine," David said. "You know I wouldn't leave Travis anywhere that wasn't safe. Besides, look who's going to be watching him," he laughed. Ali was sitting down with the kids around him showing them magic tricks with a rope. Travis was fine with it, and I told him that I would be back soon. When we got into the car of course I asked where we were going.

"We're going to see Mr. G."

Now, a normal person would have asked what the "G" stood for, but by now you know that I got this far without being inquisitive, and I wasn't about to change now. As far as I was concerned, "Mr. G" was enough until David chose to say more.

With me still being a little nervous about leaving Travis behind, we got into the car and drove a couple of hours north and into the green-covered Pocono Mountains. I had never seen—or even heard of—the Poconos before. We drove through beautiful mountains and valleys, across small rivers on quaint old covered bridges. It was maybe the most scenic place I had seen to this point. This was even more beautiful than Deer Lake. We actually had a pleasant drive, not fighting about anything. David said that this "Mr. G" guy may want to come to Las Vegas and of course I could get him in and out without anybody knowing. "You know the drill," he said.

"This is going to be a brief meeting, but if I blow my nose, excuse yourself and go to the powder room." This was actually our regular signal and I had no problem with it. I still didn't have the slightest interest in these men's business or private affairs.

Eventually we arrived in the sleepy little town of Milford, and it was like going back thirty years into the past: no crowds, clean streets with giant trees, friendly people, and a slower pace to everything. I could feel my blood pressure dropping by the minute, and I imagined that nobody who lived here ever had a stroke. Eventually we pulled up to an older home on a tree-lined street where each property seemed to sit on an acre or two.

Opening the front door to greet us was a strikingly handsome Italian man in his mid-forties. I knew he was Italian because I had met so many in Las Vegas in the last few years; they all have that look: dark brown eyes, olive skin, and usually very well dressed. This man was immaculate, with perfectly groomed salt-and-pepper hair, and wearing a starched light blue shirt under a dark sports jacket, pressed grey slacks, and a shiny gold ring on the little finger of his right hand–a pinky ring as the Italians in

Vegas called it. David introduced us.

"John, meet my lady, Franny," David said. "Franny, say Hi to my friend, John."

"It's great to meet you," John said with a big smile. "I've heard so much about you."

"Well, that's funny because I've heard nothing about you," I said. "My David never tells me anything about his friends."

"You don't know how glad that makes me," he replied as we walked into his living room. "Back in the city, where I live, people talk too much. Lots of lying. Gets them in trouble. It's not worth it."

"I couldn't agree more," I said. "I don't like people who get into other people's business."

John then turned to David and said, "I think you got a keeper here. She's terrific." We sat in the living room and John brought us drinks. We chatted about odds and ends, like my work at the Palace in Vegas and the new wax museum. John said he had some friends who worked there and he visited occasionally, but he preferred the Poconos when he had time to get away. I said I would have to agree with him, at least from what I had seen so far. He said that he had a men's club in New York and they often came up here to hunt and fish, but really just to get away. (I didn't tell him how much I hated these guys hunting and killing these poor animals just for fun. It was different if you were hungry. But I kept my mouth shut on that one.)

John (or "Mr. G") explained that his work in New York was very stressful and that he was convinced that a weekend in the country was a million times better than any psychiatrist or drugs. He thought psychiatrists were crazier than the rest of us.

I agreed with him that country life was much better than resorting to drugs or shrinks. We never had either in Campbell

County. A little moonshine was all anybody seemed to need, I told him. That led to a discussion of my daddy as a moonshiner. John/Mr. G said that he had started out in New York working for people who did the same thing, only he called them "bootleggers." He said he had never been to East Tennessee, but would love to see it one day.

David explained that I specialized in helping him make arrangements for when his friends visited Las Vegas, and that I was very discreet. I wrote down my phone number for John/Mr. G and gave it to him.

"Anytime you need help with getting a room, just give me a call," I said.

"Fantastic, I'm sure you'll be hearing from me one day," John answered. "In fact, call Franny anytime you want to reach me," David added. "She'll always know how to find me. I'm on the road a lot."

Well, after about twenty minutes of this chit chat, David in fact gave me the signal by blowing his nose, and I waited a minute or two before asking where the bathroom was. There was one in the back of the first floor, so I went in there for a few minutes, then I got bored and walked out onto the back porch where I had a smoke and walked around the large backyard. It was the second time today that I had to take a walk so that the men could talk privately. But I didn't mind at all. I just loved getting out into the woods for the first time since I left LaFollette. My life had become so chaotic that I didn't realize how much I missed those Tennessee hills.

After about twenty minutes, the men joined me outside and we said our goodbyes. I told John/Mr. G that I was anxious to see my young son who we left in Deer Lake with the Champ, whom my host seemed to know.

"Cherish that boy," he said. "I lost one of my children in an accident a couple of years ago, and to this day I regret every minute that I didn't spend with him." When he said this, I thought I noticed his eyes welling up. I gave him a big hug, said how sorry I was about his son, and that I looked forward to seeing him in Las Vegas. But he never called. It wasn't until years later that I learned that John/Mr. G was really John Gotti, the vicious "Dapper Don" Godfather of the New York Mafia. It turned out, as David later told me, that his boy died when a neighbor ran over him; the neighbor soon disappeared off the face of the earth! I also learned that the sleepy little

John Gotti

town of Milford, PA had been a Mafia getaway place for decades. Could-a fooled me.

So it was still another two-hour drive back to Deer Lake, where we picked up Travis and said goodbye to the Champ and Veronica. We saw Ali a few more times in Las Vegas, and Travis often watched Ali training there. We both sat ringside for his last fight in town, this one against reigning champion Larry Holmes. Ali was in his late thirties now, and up close you could see that the years had taken a toll. In the ring, even though he didn't appear heavy, he still lumbered around slowly, allowing Larry to punish him with many huge punches to the head—no one will ever convince me that this fight didn't play a role in Ali's later diagnosis of Parkinson's Disease.

It was sad to see how the Champ's skills had diminished over the years, and in this match his own trainer stopped the fight after the tenth round—Ali had lost every round of the fight. We could tell the Champ was disgusted with himself because when we saw him after the event he gave his fight gloves to Travis, saying while autographing them, "I doubt I'll be needing them much more." After a year or so he actually stepped into the ring one last time and lost again. Nonetheless, *Sports Illustrated* would later name Ali "Athlete of the Century," and he certainly was that and more to Travis and me. (Sadly, those autographed gloves disappeared years later along with everything else Travis had kept in a storage space that he neglected to pay the rent on. Somebody sure got lucky at a Vegas storage locker auction!)

But, back at Deer Lake long before this sad event, all was fun and games, especially for Travis. From there it was back to Newark Airport and a long flight back to Nevada. We all slept like logs after this whirlwind.

It must have been my month for meeting wiseguys because there was another major one waiting to hug me when I returned to my home in Vegas. I had met a lot of them, almost all from Chicago, when I had first arrived here, thanks in large part to my dumb luck working at that "dress shop" on East Sahara. The Lefty Rosenthals and Herbie Blitzsteins of the world were always around the shop or at our favorite after-work hangouts like the Stardust or Chicago Joe's. Although I never asked or wanted to know the details of what they did, it was understood that they weren't Boy Scout leaders. I just threw them into the same lump of people like my daddy and his friends, the moonshiners of Campbell County. And I never judged any of them. Often, they were our drinking buddies, and I have to be honest—I never felt in danger around them. I'm sure I was naïve, but that's the God's honest truth. They were all gentlemen to me and my sister, and I frankly felt more relaxed around them than I did around the slimy politicians that the Big Guy hung around with (except for President Carter, that is.)

I always knew that Fat Herbie did some business with a jewelry store, the Gold Rush, Ltd., located a few blocks from the dress shop, just off the Strip over on West Sahara, but until I returned from the Poconos, I had never met the owner of the store, which mostly sold used jewelry. Coincidentally, it turned out that this owner's cousin Elaine lived right next door to Travis and me. Elaine was already living in the neighborhood when Travis and I arrived, and it was a stroke of luck for us both because she was also a single mother raising a young son who was the same age as Travis. Elaine and I took turns looking out for the boys when the other wasn't home, and little Todd and Travis became best buddies and spent almost every day together—practically inseparable. This made me feel good, because I was spending so much time working and I was always determined that Travis never felt lonely or unhappy. Between Todd, Elaine, and my own siblings pitching in (not to mention hanging out with The President and the Champ), Travis's childhood was pretty darned good.

Like almost everybody else in this crazy place, Elaine was from Chicago, so I always had it in the back of my mind that she might be "connected," just like every other Chicago transplant I managed to meet. To me, it was a reasonable assumption. Little did I know that one of her Chicago cousins—the man I was about to meet—was not only connected, but he would end up being the key reason that the Chicago Outfit's long reign in Vegas came crashing down.

Anyway, Elaine and I were out front one day shooting the breeze, when a shiny black Cadillac pulled up to her house. I knew something was up when a handsome, dark-haired man and a pretty blonde got out of the backseat while his driver stayed behind the wheel. Until now, the only limos seen in this neighborhood were those of my David. Elaine introduced me to her cousin, Tony, and his wife Nancy, and invited me over to join them for drinks. Tony was a stereotypical Italian from that era, just like a younger version of John Gotti, but loaded down with gold chains, a shiny watch, and *two* pinky rings.

Tony and I chatted for a while about Fat Herbie and our other mutual acquaintances like his partner Lefty Rosenthal over at the Stardust and local lawyer Oscar Goodman, who seemed to represent every Chicagoan in Vegas, Tony included.

(L-R) Tony Spilotro, Oscar Goodman, and Herbie Blitzstein

"Tony and Nancy have had a place down on Sahara, but they're looking to move farther away from the Strip," Marie told me. "Since you know everybody in town and your sister is into real estate, could you let us know if you hear of a nice house that comes on the market?"

"I'll be happy to," I replied.

Before the visit ended, Tony invited me to stop by the Gold Rush, which he ran with his brother Michael, for a special discount.

"Anybody who takes care of my little nephew Todd gets special treatment at my store," he said.

I never made it to the Gold Rush, but I seemed to run into Tony Spilotro regularly over the next few years at our favorite nightspots, especially Chicago Joe's (Jan and I were there practically every other day discussing our love lives.) To me, Tony just seemed like another fun-loving guy, the kind you meet in Vegas all the time. However, his name soon began popping up on the nightly news, being accused of this or that, but I didn't pay any attention to it at the time. Again, not my business. I just assumed he was a gambler with a problem. I knew that there was some kind of a trial, but Tony was acquitted of all charges. And soon after that, our favorite waiter at Chicago Joe's appeared on TV being perp-walked in handcuffs—it turned out that Jeremiah was a major hit man for the Tony's crew, The Hole in the Wall Gang.

Anyway, after the meeting with Ali, I had returned to Las Vegas with wonderful memories and a new respect for the Big Guy. I guess I was also confused about whether I was *in love* with him, or just loved him—like a good friend with benefits. But I hated to admit that to myself, and was even more afraid to let him know. I suppose I began to be subconsciously concerned about whether there were other women like me in the other towns he visited. It wasn't like me to think such things because I always just lived in the present, but as soon as romance raises its ugly head you start to think differently. I hated myself for even thinking like a smitten schoolgirl. It was about as strange a relationship as you can imagine. He was obviously becoming obsessed with me, but was too controlling. I was falling for him (I think), but I also craved my freedom. On top of all that, we continued fighting about the same old things, his jealousy being number one, and his planning my life out for me without discussing things with me being second. Sometimes he would call me ten times in one day. We were both a mess.

"Your name is on the White House VIP list," David

informed me in one of these calls. "You are now officially on the National Committee for the Re-Election of President Carter. There will be a press kit sent to you explaining everything. You're going to be very busy."

But I was already very busy! Again he was planning my life out for the next few months.

He continued on:

"Your first assignment," he instructed, "is to help organize a $1,000 a plate dinner for the President."

"Now, David, who the Hell is going to eat a $1,000 worth of food?" I asked naïvely.

He roared with laughter.

"I love seeing things through your eyes," he said. "It's a breath of fresh air. The $1,000 is a contribution, it's not for the food."

"How much traveling is this going to take?"

"Well," he said, "I can tell you that we will be going back to the White House soon for a private luncheon given to the people that are on the Committee."

Wow! (What am I going to wear? was my first thought.) After getting my education on why you charge $1,000 a plate for dinner, it all made sense: it's all about money, not the food. I became even more intrigued with politics, and I kept the news on TV all the time. I soon knew the names and titles of all the Democratic players that might turn up at this bash. David was impressed with how fast I caught on to the game of politics and campaign fundraising.

In February of 1980, I indeed returned to the White House with David for a private luncheon given by the President and First Lady to thank the people on the Re-Election Committee. This time we brought Travis—there was no way he was going to miss another opportunity to meet a President of the United States. The luncheon was held in a section of the White House run by the US Navy called "The Mess," where everyone who prepared and served the meals was dressed in Navy uniforms. When we were escorted to The Mess, Press Secretary Jody Powell took Travis on a private tour of the White House. I was so happy that he was having experiences as a child that I never came close to having. Hell, when I was his age I was lucky to get a tour of the

Travis and me with David in front of the White House

grocery store every six months after walking for two hours to get there. I never even heard the word "limo" until I moved to Vegas.

There were people at the luncheon from different states, and we were all seated at this very long table to await the arrival of

Me, Travis, and Jody Powell

the President and First Lady. David and I were shown to the end of the table. When the Carters were announced and seated at the head of the table, I found myself sitting on the right hand side of Mr. Carter, and of course David was sitting next to me. I'm sure David arranged for me to sit right next to the President just to see what might happen. He and the President chit-chatted like longtime friends for a bit, then he introduced me to Jimmy for the second time.

"Mr. President, do you remember my assistant, Fran

Comer?" David asked. "She was here with Liza Minnelli."

"Of course," Carter answered. "She asked me about Watermelon Day in Atlanta. How have you been?" the President asked me.

"Just fine," I said. He thanked me for joining the Re-election Committee, and as he spoke I realized how good it felt having someone with a strong Southern accent achieve this status, because I was constantly being humiliated about the way I talked. So I wasn't nervous at all around "Jimmy," but I did make sure I used the proper forks and spoons (another thing David taught me.)

Everything was going well when David jokingly whispered in my ear, "No ash trays," which quickly became our private little laugh everywhere we went. "Yeah," I whispered back, "but look at the silverware!" I knew that would get him!

"Don't even think about it!" he said. "I'll get you your souvenirs!"

By the time dessert arrived—and by the way, this time the food was great—I was really loosening up and enjoying this whole thing. All at once the President of the United States leaned over and whispered in my ear, "How are you enjoying the White House?" To which I whispered back into his ear: "Can you believe this? I done come from a shithouse to the White House!" Jimmy quickly grabbed his napkin and put it up to his mouth to hide the laughter![4] He proceeded to share my answer with the First Lady and she giggled when she looked at me. I realized after I said it that I shouldn't have said "shit" but I couldn't take it back now. David is watching all this laughter but has no idea what it was about. I didn't tell him until we were in the limo.

---

[4] I'm surprised he didn't say "Me, too!" The President was also raised in a situation that required the use of an outhouse by his Plains, Georgia family.

"You said that?" he said. He roared so hard with laughter that he lost his breath and went into a coughing spell. "Black Cat, you got more balls than a pool table!" he said. It was a phrase he would repeat to me many, many times thereafter.

One night not long after, I was back in Washington once again with Travis, while David had a stay-over in New York. Rita Jenrette dropped by our hotel to slum it with Travis and I, watching movies and ordering pizza—her husband was out of town also, probably chasing some bimbo, I thought. I'll never forget the sight of her at our door, all decked out in that soon-to-be-famous floor-length mink coat and mink hat that she wore over her dripping wet blonde hair. (She had just gotten showered before she raced over.) After Travis crawled into bed, we two girls hit the champagne and had a silly old time. We eventually conked out on the giant queen-sized bed with Travis between us (he bragged about sleeping with Rita Jenrette for years afterwards.)

The next morning Rita headed home, but in fifteen minutes she called me, hysterical: John had been detained at the airport before she could get there, she said. Some law enforcement people had escorted him to their car. She was devastated.

"Franny, don't say anything," Rita cried. "My phones are tapped! They're charging John in some kind of government sting operation. Turn on the TV. It's on every channel."

It sure was. John Jenrette had been one of many politicians caught up in an FBI sting called ABSCAM, where these FBI agents had dressed up like rich Arab sheiks and secretly filmed various officials, including seven members of Congress, accepting cash for political favors. The sting had been ongoing for two years and involved over one hundred FBI agents.

Now there were a hundred reporters camped out on Rita's lawn and she was all alone and quickly becoming even more hysterical. I told her to calm down and that I'd come over to get her. She gave me her address on North Carolina Avenue, about ten blocks from the Capitol Building. When we hung up I called Marty, David's CIA friend whose number I had always kept in case of an emergency. He appeared at our hotel in a flash, and together with Travis we hopped into a hotel limo and raced over to Rita's, where we had to shove our way to her front door.

Once inside, I gave her a big hug, but typically for me, I asked no questions. None of my business. Rita asked us to get her away from the house and the press. "No problem," Marty said. I helped her put together a small suitcase and we were out the door. Marty ran the gauntlet for us, pushing aside the paparazzi like my daddy used to push aside twigs on our Sunday hikes. He told the driver to sit in the passenger side because he was driving. Travis, Rita, and I jumped into the back seat, and the race was on. The press people tried to follow us but Marty ducked into some tunnels at breakneck speed and left them in the dust. Again, I thought of daddy, and how he used to run from the revenuers down Thunder Road.

Rita and I held our breaths, but Travis was having a blast. He was one lucky kid alright. How many seven-year-olds get to have a getaway with a CIA agent as a driver? Rita stayed at my hotel until her husband showed up. From there, the Jenrettes went off with Marty. I checked in with David by phone as soon as they were gone.

"I can't leave you alone for a minute," he chided me. He suggested, and I immediately agreed, that Travis and I get our butts back to Vegas immediately. He would come to DC and find out what was going on with John Jenrette.

When I returned to Las Vegas, Rita called and told me that John was accused of taking a fifty thousand dollar bribe. But she said that the whole thing was a huge set-up and that together they were going to fight this thing. I wished her well, and told her not to hesitate to call if she needed anything. She said that David had already been a huge help. According to what Rita told me over the following months, she knew in her heart that John was innocent. Although I didn't say it, I felt otherwise. I was always a pretty good judge of character, and I never liked the look of this man. The sex must have been blinding because it certainly blinded Rita.

She decided to do anything and sell anything in order to help finance John's legal bills for the upcoming fall trial. There were lawn sales, car sales, motorcycle sales, paid interviews—anything to help. She even said she was trying to sell her infamous fur coat (don't know if she ever did.)

Of course, I was in no position to criticize Rita since my own relationship with David was no walk in the park. His obsession with me only seemed to increase (he was still calling me ten times a day), and I was torn between going along with it and trying to find a way out. Ugh. We began to argue more frequently, but we always seemed to patch things up. I was torn because I had feelings for David and I was thankful for the security he provided Travis and me—not to mention all the "whirlwinds." But the fights continued and even escalated. At the same time, I began to worry that my brother Bobby was getting too close to David. He really began looking up to David as some sort of mentor or father figure and was often performing odd jobs for him, jobs that I knew no details about. I knew that David was a powerful man and I had seen glimpses of violence, so I wondered what sort of "jobs" my brother might be performing; I worried that my boyfriend would land my brother back in jail.

David's jealousy was also an issue. It worsened when he drank, and he was drinking more and more as time went on. One night while I was with him in his regular suite at Caesar's, he started getting especially bullying, demanding to know the names of every man I knew—the guy I spoke to in the lobby, the guy on the elevator, blah, blah, blah. While he sat there in his underwear with a glass of Scotch in his hand, I got my things together and headed for the door.

"I'm outa' here," I said.

"No, you're not!" David ordered.

He then got up and blocked the door—a bad move that only caused Black Cat Marcum to emerge. (I'm reminded of the Hulk's expression: "You won't like me when I'm mad!") We started into a pulling and pushing match, and I don't think David knew what hit him—he had only heard stories of my legendary dustups, but had never seen me in action. We fell back onto the bed and I was able to kick his drunken butt to the floor before I made my way out the door. As I was running down the hall, my brother Bob was headed in the other direction towards the room. I suppose he was there to see if David had any more "work" for him.

"Bob, you'd better tell him what will happen if he continues to get in my business," I told him before he could get to the room. "And he'd better not follow me home." Bob knew very well what I was capable of, having seen me in action back in LaFollette and elsewhere.

I arrived downstairs and was giving my car ticket to the bell captain when I heard a commotion behind me on the casino floor. I turned and saw David stumbling between the one-armed bandits while trying to pull his pants up from his ankles, with my brother trailing behind him with the rest of his clothes. Now I was laughing hysterically. All I could think of was: "I'd give anything for Jimmy Carter or Teddy Kennedy to see David now."

The two of them made it to the bell captain's station where I was standing, still waiting for my car to show up; I wonder if they took their good old time finding it so that David and I could keep the show going. If that was the bell captain's plan, it worked. David slumped onto a little retaining wall that bordered one of Caesar's fountains, but he continued yelling at me about all of my alleged boyfriends. When he didn't shut up I walked over to him.

"Don't say I didn't warn you," I said as I pushed him over backwards right into the fountain pool, which was about five-feet deep. With the crowd gathered around us applauding me, my brother Bob jumped in and pulled David—but not his pants—out. There he stood with the family jewels on prominent display.

"Are you crazy, Black Cat?" my brother yelled. "He's drunk. He could've drowned!"

"He's lucky," I said. "I at least warned him, and you know I never do that."

By this time, my car had arrived—the very car David had bought for me. I gave the carhop a $20 bill and drove off home. The sight in my rear view mirror, this advisor to presidents and celebrities dripping wet in his underwear, made me laugh so hard I could hardly drive. Not five minutes after I had returned home, I heard the doorbell ring and I knew exactly who it was: I opened the front door to see a still dripping wet David standing there. I was bursting out laughing inside, but I managed to put on a stern face and, without allowing him in, told him to go back to Caesar's and sober up. Through the window I watched him stumble back into Caesar's Courtesy Car, where the backseat must have felt like a wet sponge by now.

The next day, after the effects wore off, he was a different person, laughing his ass off about the whole incident. Although it was the perfect excuse to end the relationship, I forgave him nonetheless; I was so conflicted. By now I was certain that I loved David but was not *in love* with him. Big difference. But this is the way it was during these years. I was confusing the two emotions and piling that on top of the fears I had—for a variety of reasons—of breaking up with him.

We had a rip-roaring fight in September 1980 when David dropped a bombshell on me. After visiting with David's client Shirley MacLaine in her Malibu home (and talking her out of some clothes for the wax museum), we arrived at LA's Hyatt Hotel, where David had booked a suite so we could be near the Beverly Hilton Hotel. There, we were to help manage that $1000-a-plate fundraising dinner for President Carter.

Jan and Jerry were also staying at the Hyatt–they had flown in from Vegas to attend the dinner with us (Jerry loved rubbing elbows with celebrities.) Jan volunteered to help me make sure all the VIPs were taken care of.

Before leaving for the Hilton, David and I were relaxing in our suite when he let it slip. I was ironing a blouse that I was going to wear when David took a phone call that sounded pretty strange—something about his mother-in-law visiting Florida for his son's birthday—what the Hell? A mother-in-law usually means a wife, and this was the first thing I had even heard about a "son." After hanging up, David nonchalantly sat on down on the bed and began telling me about what his son was doing.

"David, you are divorced aren't you?" I asked. "Because

that conversation didn't sound like it." I could tell by the look on his face what the answer was.

He sat there on the edge of the bed, staring down at the floor, then sheepishly said, "No, but I only see her twice a year because she's still my responsibility."

At which point I lost it.

"You son of a bitch!" I screamed. "You've been lying to me all this time? How could you do that to me?"

"C'mon, Franny, you know I love you," he said. "Do you think I would have given you all the things I have with no future in sight?"

"But that's not the point," I fumed. "You led me to believe you were a single man. You were leading two lives, and taking me along for the ride!"

"Quit acting like a raving bitch," he shot back. "I've given you everything any woman could want!"

My temper now went from zero to one hundred in an instant. At the same time that I realized I still had that hot iron in my hand, and without thinking I took that thing and planted it right on his back.

"Mother fuck!" he screamed before running into the bathroom, where he jumped into the shower to try and cool down his burn. He locked the door behind him but that didn't stop me from unloading a barrage of four-letter words at the top of my lungs. While this was going on, my sister Jan and her husband Jerry arrived and were knocking on the door. However, we didn't hear them right away—we were too busy going to war.

"You cocksucker! How dare you keep that from me," I yelled through the bathroom door. "I told you what I went through with Dan—how I beat his bitch half to death! Now you tell me that *I'm that bitch?*"

For a minute David said nothing, he just stood in that shower moaning softly. Eventually I stopped screaming and the water stopped running.

"I'm sorry," David said through the bathroom door. "I thought you knew. My wife and I are only together for our children. There's nothing there, I promise. When the kids go off to college in the next two years the marriage will be over. I was going to wait until then to ask you to marry me."

I slumped backwards onto the bed to take it all in; I was touched that he felt that strongly about me. However the feelings weren't mutual—I had no intention of marrying David. He was too controlling, and I could only take him in small doses. There was no way I was racing into a marriage with this man. Eventually both my temper and his burn cooled down.

"It's OK to come out," I told him. "I'm sorry I lost it."

When David emerged from the bathroom, we hugged. When my hand touched his back he yelled out in pain. I looked at the bright red patch on his back and wished I had some of the polk weed from my Tennessee garden to put on it. He asked me to call the concierge and have some A&D ointment sent up, along with some tape and gauze. After that call he took some aspirin while we continued grumbling a bit, but at the same time continued getting ready for this event that he would attend with a perfect iron burn right on his back.

By now Jan and Jerry were downright pounding on the door, so I got up to let them in after David went back into the bathroom with his clothes in hand.

"We've been knocking for ten minutes," Jan said. "What the hell was going on?"

"Sorry, David was in the shower and I had the TV up loud," I lied.

"It didn't sound like the television to us," Jerry said.

"Well, what can I say? David should be out in a minute and we'll head down."

The ointment arrived and, without letting Jerry or Jan see it, I took it to David in the bathroom. When David finally emerged, we both pretended everything was wonderful; we never let anyone know we had fights. We made our way downstairs and had drinks in the lobby bar (David had a double, straight up) while waiting for the limo to pick us up to take us to the Hilton.

Upon arriving at the fundraiser, I knew right away this was going to be another whirlwind experience. The place was a beehive of activity, with me and my new friends on the Re-Election Committee getting things ready before the VIPs showed up. After we set up our greeting station and coordinated with the other volunteers, the first of 400 guests began to arrive. I had never seen anything like this: stretch limos were snaked around the block, waiting to drop off movie stars, famous politicians, trophy wives—you name it. Once they made it into the lobby there was one army of waiters and waitresses, another army of Secret Service agents, and a third army of LAPD watching the proceedings like hawks. There was so much law enforcement on the scene that I was wondering when Fate Thomas was going to show up.

The first thing I saw them do was to sweep the ballroom for bombs. I also played a small role in helping security; one of my main responsibilities was working at the entrance to the ballroom, checking the IDs of all the guests against the invitation list that had been submitted to the Secret Service some time earlier. Those agents watched over my shoulder as I verified each guest. These were the days before metal detectors and "wands," so we had to be extra careful that no one entered the ballroom that wasn't invited.

The President arrived (along with more Secret Service) with Teddy Kennedy, California Governor Jerry Brown and Universal Pictures chief Lew Wasserman. They were quickly taken to a holding room while the ballroom filled up with the guests, some of whom were escorted to the private suite to meet with the President.

In the lobby, poor David spent time pressing the flesh with the guests—looking for new clients, I suppose. I cringed every time someone walked up to David to pat him on the back. Whenever that happened he looked at me and flinched. Eventually we took our seats and the PA system blared a recording of "Hail to the Chief," as the President entered the room with Teddy. I remember in his presentation, President Carter criticizing the Republican candidate Ronald Reagan, saying something to the effect that he would be too prone to start wars if he were elected.

The bottom line for me was that the event went off without a hitch, which impressed David to no end. After we ate our $1000 worth of food, we made our way back to the Hyatt, where David, still in pain, got understandably plastered in the hotel bar. After the booze took hold, he again got around to the subject of our relationship. I told him that as far as marriage was concerned, we'd cross that bridge in a couple of years. In the meantime, I suggested that we keep things the way they were, and he reluctantly agreed. Then he told me a funny story.

"Remember when we were sitting in the front row for the Norton fight a couple of years ago?" he asked.

"How could I forget?" I said. "For a minute I thought he

recognized me and was going to jump over the ropes to yell at me again for confusing him with Spinks!"

"Well, the thing was, my wife was watching the fight that night at home and saw me sitting with you," David said. "The next day she called me and asked me who was 'that woman you were sitting next to?' I told her, 'That's Ken Norton's girlfriend. He wanted me to sit with her to keep her company and watch out for her.'"

"David, couldn't you have come up with another story?" I asked. "Why did you have to say *him*, of all people?" He just laughed.

"It seemed to be the right thing to say," he said.

David's controlling ways didn't end with his shoulder blade getting torched, and as time went on it was obvious that his interest in me was still more like obsession. I know I should have stopped it right then in LA, just like I should have when I pushed him into Caesar's fountains, but I was in too deep. I had confused feelings about him. They were strong, but a bit short of love. I was a wreck.

Rita & John Jenrette. She stood by him for longer than he deserved, as things turned out

At least I wasn't alone in my misery. In October 1980, a month after the Hilton fundraiser, John Jenrette was convicted, and his loyal wife Rita called me in tears, worried about the future. But her resolve was still firm and she went into overdrive to sell whatever she had left in order to pay for John's appeal. She sold a mild "tell-all" to the *Washington Post* called "Diary of a Mad Congresswife," but then shocked all of us when she sold some skin to *Playboy Magazine*. "We just needed the money," she told me. John had also teased her by telling her that no one would want to look at her thirty-year-old body, so she decided to call his bluff. The issue wouldn't hit until March, and much would happen before then.

I'll never forget Rita's call that came just after New Year's 1981. She was howling mad and using so many four-letter words that I thought I was listening to a recording of me.

"That mother-fucking son-of-a-bitch!" she screamed into the phone. I assumed that she must have been talking about one of John's prosecutors.

"Jesus, Rita, what's going on?" I asked. I had never heard her sound like this.

"He's guilty! That bastard is guilty!"

"Guilty of what? What—I mean who—are you talking about?"

"John!" she screamed. "He took the money just like they said he did. I was going through the closet to see what we could sell, when fat rolls of hundred-dollar bills fell out of his suede loafers. I counted $25,000. To top it off, he's out of town, allegedly on business, but the number he gave me is a fake. His lawyer told me he's in Florida. Did I tell you he has an ex-girlfriend in Florida? At least I thought she was an ex."

"Holy shit," I said, pretending to be surprised. "What are you going to do?"

"You mean after I throw all his crap in the dumpster?" she asked. "I'm going to have the divorce papers in front of him before he can pour another Brandy Alexander." And that's exactly what Rita did. During their divorce negotiations, John had the gall to ask Rita for alimony, but both Rita and the presiding judge laughed at that one. Hell hath no fury...

My own David made a troubling admission to me some months later, but it was one that really didn't shock me: it turned out that Jenrette had asked him to lie to Rita about the Florida trip—to cover for him by saying he had set up a business trip for him down south, when he was really with a woman. It was just more evidence to me that honest men are almost impossible to find.

John Jenrette was able to postpone his two-year sentence until 1985, and then he served out thirteen months. In 1989 he was convicted of shoplifting a tie and some shoes from a department store in Bailey's Crossroads, Virginia. Somehow, John is still a lawyer and in the PR biz. He remarried years ago and spends six months of the year in South Carolina and the other six in Florida.

Now Rita really landed on her feet—that's for sure. First she wrote an exposé of life in Washington entitled *My Capitol Secrets*, then she moved to New York where she became a series-three broker on Wall Street. When she lived in the city she dated comedian Dan Ackroyd. About this time we lost touch with each other, but later I learned that she got a degree from Harvard Business School before landing a job at an international real estate firm. She also became very active in a number of charities. When Rita was working on a real estate deal in Italy in 2003, she met Italian Prince Nicolò Boncompagni Ludvisi, whom she eventually married. So Rita is now Principessa Rita Boncompagi Ludvisi, living in a lavish Roman villa. Way to go, girl!

Chapter Five

Battles on Many Fronts

RITA AND JOHN WERE FIGHTING IT OUT in Washington, David and I were arguing in LA, and violent labor unions had Las Vegas under siege. It seemed like the world had turned upside-down, and I had no control over anything.

In the meantime, brother Bob wanted to get married to a seventeen-year-old girl, but the girl's father wouldn't go for it. However, since she was only a few months from turning eighteen they made wedding plans anyway. David and I bought their rings, paid for the wedding, and wished the best for them. And of course it wasn't long before she was pregnant. I was in LA when Bob and his new wife gave birth to a beautiful baby boy back in Las Vegas. David flew in to see them when the baby was born and I made the eight-hour drive that I had done so often that I knew every turn in the road by heart.

On top of everything else, I had taken on charity work because I enjoyed helping youngsters in need. It brought me great satisfaction to hold fundraisers to help less fortunate children instead of sleazy politicians who just acted like children. I really enjoyed organizing committees and volunteers to raise money for this and other needy causes. David loved the idea that I was doing this and even helped out if I needed something that seemed difficult to obtain or achieve, since he knew someone in every walk of life. Lots of times I repaid his contacts by comp-ing them to a show in

Vegas—I had plenty of what we called "Power of the Pen."

It seemed my life couldn't be more insane and hectic. Looking back, I wonder where I got the energy to live it! And I still had this knack for accidentally meeting people who were connected to inside information. One day at one of my children's charity functions I met an older lady who seemed lonely. She was very sweet and willing to help out with anything we asked, but I felt sorry for her so I tried to give her a little more attention. Come to find out, she worked as a secretary for the local field office of the FBI. When I told David about her he said: "You hit the jackpot! Take her out, comp her to some shows in town, and get to know her as much as you can. Find out if she's able to run a scope on people. This could come in handy when I bring people into town." By "scope," David meant seeing what the FBI had in its background check files on an individual. Well, I did find out and my new friend did have access to these files, and she was willing to access them for us. She just had to be careful, but she was willing to do this for me. I can't remember all the names David wrote down for me to give to her, but I knew that some were in the notorious "Black Book," people barred from ever stepping foot in a casino due to their criminal past.

So, for the next few months she would periodically hand me a manila envelope stuffed thick with photocopies of FBI files. I never looked at them (not my business), but David would tell me how useful they were especially for the casino owners who now knew which of their places had government "bugs" (hidden microphones) in them. David also told me that the wiseguys who remained in town were most thankful to me for this information, and should I ever need anything–blah, blah, blah. But I had never gone there and never would.

This secretary ended up calling me all the time; I guess she had felt she had found a new best friend. She knew nothing about my background except that I could get her into any show on the Strip for free, and she wanted to see them all; she told me that she could never afford to do this on her salary, and she was ecstatic to have the best seat to the best, and most expensive, shows in town. I liked making someone happy, besides it was just a show. No big deal to me, but a big deal to her—and an even bigger deal to David's secretive clients.

With all that was going on in my world, I felt like I needed a couple of weeks back in the quiet Tennessee hills just to get away from it all. More and more bodies were being found in the desert, thanks to the union organizers clashing with the non-unionists and the Chicago Outfit. Since the Nevada Palace had finally re-opened with Gene Lucas now in charge, I was back there working more than I had been recently, and I wasn't about to take orders from some union goon—despite the fact that my car was still getting egged and my tires slashed. But for years we had been lucky: other places (and people) in town were getting blown up. Our luck finally ran out when the problems of another Palace employee, one I had trained a couple of years earlier, made me forget about my vandalized car.

Not long after Gene Lucas had taken over, he asked me if I would train a new manager to run the hotel so that I could concentrate on my work as group sales director. The new guy's name was Gene Ritchie, and he was another out-of-towner with no understanding of this crazy city. He also resented a woman training him, so we butted heads quite a few times. I tried my best to help him, but he was what I refer to as "a know-it-all male." Of course, he was now up against Black Cat Marcum, and

God knows I wasn't going to take any putdowns from this guy. So it was a pretty contentious period.

What made it worse was the fact that the GM made Ritchie and I share an office. At this time, in a futile attempt to get me to fall in love with him, David was sending roses to my desk every week, and of course Ritchie, the new guy, complained about it; he didn't like the smell of roses—they took up too much room, etc., The truth is that he just wanted to aggravate me.

"If you don't like it, go piss up a rope," I snapped back at him one day. "I've been here too long to listen or take any bullshit from the likes of you." Ritchie's attitude eventually pushed us all to the point of not wanting to help him anymore. He thought he knew everything. Well, fuck him—let's allow this jerk enough rope to hang himself. Of course, we never for a minute imagined what eventually happened.

Not long after his arrival on the scene, Ritchie got mixed up with a prostitute named Sheri, the founder of the famous brothels Sheri's Crystal Palace in Nye County and Sheri's Ranch in Pahrump, about an hour west of town. He actually brought Sheri to a Christmas party at Gene Lucas's home, introducing her with a phony name, "Diana." But everybody at the party had been in Vegas so long that they all knew who she really was. The next day at work I told Ritchie that we were all very familiar with "Diana," and what she did for a living. Now I was no prude. In fact, I knew many of the "working girls" (prostitutes) and even allowed some of them to conduct their "business" in our rooms. But I screened them carefully to make sure these were independent girls with no pimps or drug issues. But I also knew that some of the big brothels had hidden owners and a history of scandals, gunplay and payoffs.

I had it on good authority that "connected" guys from Florida had their hooks in most of them. These whorehouses were not places for the managers of major hotels to hang their hats.

Although I had long since stopped giving advice to this ungrateful lout, I decided to make an exception.

"You'd better be careful there," I warned him. "Just because it's called 'Sheri's Ranch' doesn't mean she's the owner. She's just another working girl. Other people own those brothels, and besides, you have two little boys—this is not somebody you want around your children."

I didn't stop there: "You need to know whose toes you might be stepping on. You're not from here. Vegas is different from other places."

Typically, Ritchie took offense to my advice.

"Mind your own business, Franny," Ritchie said. "I'm a grown man and I don't need advice from someone with a mother complex."

"Fine," I said. "Then screw you and the horse you rode in on. Just don't come crying to 'mother' when you fuck up." I thought to myself that I never should have gone against my own instincts to allow this jerk to learn his lessons the hard way. Well, he must have done just that, because a few months later when I was sitting with friends in one of my favorite Vegas watering holes, the bartender stopped by to tell me that Gene Ritchie had left a message for me earlier in the day, before I had arrived. He said it was an emergency and that I should call immediately. I couldn't imagine any emergency that would involve me, the PR Director; I was merely responsible for promoting the hotel. There were people in place to handle day-to-day problems.

When I finally got around to calling him I learned that the emergency had nothing to do with the hotel, but Gene sounded panicked as he began to tell me this long, incoherent story, which I interrupted after a few minutes.

"Gene, forget the details, just what do you want from me?" I asked.

"There's a contract out on me," he said in a shaking voice I had never heard before. "And maybe you can help me—I was told you were connected."

"I don't know what you're talking about," I said. "Besides you're not important enough for that kind of stuff, and if this was true you wouldn't even know it. Someone's trying to scare you. Who did you piss off now?"

Of course, his story was that he hadn't done anything wrong, but I told him that I specifically remembered warning him about stepping on the wrong toes and he obviously didn't listen. He had accused me of having a "mother" complex, and now here he was crying on my shoulder like a ten-year-old who just met the school bully. Like a good mother I eventually calmed him down and we hung up. Back at home I called the Big Guy and I told him about Ritchie's "emergency."

"See if you hear anything," I said. "I don't think it's true, but Vegas is getting dangerous these days."

"Isn't that the guy you trained, who then turned into a complete asshole towards you?" David asked.

"Yes," I said, "but he's just stupid. I wouldn't want this to be true because he has two little boys." But within two weeks Gene Ritchie completely disappeared off the face of the earth. His poor family never saw him again. Despite the lack of evidence, everybody in my circle was pretty certain about what became of the Nevada Palace's manager: like dozens before him, he was almost certainly spending the rest of eternity taking a dirt nap a few miles outside of town in the Nevada desert.

I felt very bad, but there was nothing I could have done. This was Las Vegas in the 1980s. Things were taking a new turn, and Sin City had become much more violent and didn't have the small town flavor it had when the Rat Pack entertained us and the gangsters kept things running smoothly and seemed to know everybody personally. In those days it was mostly stoolies and cheats that were on the receiving end of the violence. Now, anybody could be a target: cab drivers, waiters, hotel personnel, prostitutes' boyfriends—anybody.

Ritchie wasn't the last Palace employee to disappear either. Out of left field in February 1989, previous owner Bob Mariscal, who I thought had no business with the Palace anymore, came by when I just happened to be there and said, "Tell Jim Schiff I'll get his money later. I don't have it today." I had no idea what he was talking about, so I told him that I thought he should tell Jim himself. But he insisted that I had to do it, so I called Jim and told him the story, and he was not happy—to put it mildly.

"My money better get here in two days," he yelled into the phone. "Have you been depositing their money?"

"What money?" I asked. Apparently Mariscal owed the hotel on a bad debt.

"Tell Bob I want my money today," Jim said.

"OK," I replied. I resented being in the middle of all this, especially as someone uninterested in money and having absolutely no idea what anyone was talking about.

Soon, other people began calling the hotel looking for Mariscal, but I hadn't heard from him and had no answers for them.

Eventually Jim told me that Mariscal's abandoned Lincoln Continental had been found in the parking lot of Jerry's Nugget Casino in North Las Vegas. The police came by to interview us, but we knew nothing—at least I didn't. And I assumed that just like Gene Ritchie and so many others, Mariscal's body would never turn up. But in this case I was wrong: nine months later Bob Mariscal's decomposed body was found in the desert (which was fast turning into the unofficial city cemetery), seven miles north of town.

I remember hearing the news from his bookkeeper on the day the body was found.

"Franny, are you sitting down?" he asked. I wasn't but I lied.

"Bob Mariscal was found dead," he told me in a shaking voice.

"What?"

"I'm sure you'll hear about it on the news," he said. "I don't know what's going to happen now, but I'll call you back when I know more."

I was obviously stunned by this news, but the biggest shock was to follow. I immediately called Jim, who said he already knew. He told me that Mariscal had bullet wounds to his head and torso, but that it wasn't a robbery—all of his cash and jewelry were still on him. It was obviously a Vegas-style revenge killing, and soon it was all over the news. Of course, no one was ever even arrested for the murder. I certainly have no idea which of Mariscal's many debts had led to his killing, but the word was that he allegedly had problems with gangsters in LA and with a local mortgage company partnership he had supposedly defrauded out of millions—in addition to what he owed the Palace.

Anyway, after Gene Ritchie's disappearance I returned to Los Angeles. David called me there and said, "I'm sending Bob [my brother] and his wife and baby to stay with you. I don't like the idea of you being alone there. You're too trusting." It was clear that David wanted my brother in the Brentwood house not only for my security, but also as a way to keep an eye on me. Since he was paying the mortgage it was entirely his call. I was in no position to argue with him, and I definitely was unready to give up the condo.

So sure enough, Bob & family arrived at the Barrington Avenue house and of course I fell in love with their baby, Robbie—the parents got on my nerves, but the baby made up for it. By now I had learned not to discuss anything about my private business in front of these two since I knew they would tell David everything. The two men were as thick as thieves by now and I knew that Bob was telling the Big Guy every move I made, big and little.

I remember one night when David called me from Brazil and told me that he knew exactly what I wore that day. That pissed me off because it told me that my brother was giving him every small detail he could about me. David didn't care that I was fuming—he wanted to let me know he had ways of knowing my every move. It was intimidation, pure and simple, and it was really eating away at me. Of course, I was never one to hide my anger, so the tactic only caused David and me to fight even more. He even opened an office in LA, which of course meant he'd be spending more time here breathing down my neck. I felt trapped.

The question I kept asking myself was: why couldn't David have been honest with me about his wife and family? Now, with the trust issue added to the control issue, I thought it was more than fair for me to have my own second life—I had finally realized that this situation didn't hold any future for me. Traveling, gifts, money and excitement did not overcome what I was feeling, so I told David that I was going to start seeing other people. That did not go over well—in fact he was furious and warned me not to go there because it might end up ugly. Now I took that as a threat, and I don't like that. Even though I was a little frightened I would never show it—I knew he would sense it and use it against me.

Despite everything, we continued seeing each other (although now non-exclusively, to my mind.) It was hard for both of us to completely let go since we shared so many memories and experiences. Besides, every time we had a fight, David would go out and buy me an expensive gift, like a three-karat diamond he gave me after one particularly nasty blow-up. I was reluctant to accept it, but what girl is going to turn down "a girl's best friend" that big? I was totally conflicted, simultaneously getting very dissatisfied yet still seduced by the perks of this crazy relationship. And I still traveled to meet David in New York, Washington, or elsewhere.

One of the few constants in my life was my regular gabfest with Jan at Chicago Joe's; no matter what dramas we were living, we always made time to catch up on each other's lives. One day in 1986 we were in a booth seated right across from Oscar Goodman and Tony Spilotro. I walked over to say "Hi."

Chicago Joe's Restaurant

"How's the kid sister doing?" Tony asked. "You two looked mighty serious over there."

"Oh, we're still trying to find our way through this life," I said and laughed it off.

"Hey, Franny," Tony continued, "I'm going to Chicago for a week, call me when I get back, and we'll talk over your *problems*." He winked and laughed, obviously flirting with me.

"I'm sure you could fix my *problems*," I flirted back. "Too bad you're going out of town, I was looking for something to do this weekend."

"*Accidenti*—I have to go to Chicago to get some dental work done," he explained.

"We do have dentists out here, you know," I suggested.

"None as good as my brother, Patsy," Tony explained. "He's the only one I let near my pearly whites. I wouldn't let one of these dumb motherfuckers touch me."

"Actually, I know what you mean," I replied. "You know that if you ever get sick, you'd better go to Scripps in California."

"Yeah, but at least Vegas has good attorneys," he said, and we all looked at Oscar, laughing. "And they're more important than doctors these days."

We laughed and said our goodbyes. It was the last time we ever flirted with each other. In fact, it was the last time I ever saw Tony Spilotro. Like Gene Ritchie, he just disappeared. However, unlike Ritchie, Tony's body eventually turned up alongside his brother Michael's, buried in a shallow grave in an Indiana cornfield, found by a farmer applying pesticide to his crops. I heard that his face was beaten so badly that it didn't even look human. Ironically, few of his precious "pearly whites" remained in place. However, those that survived led to the positive identification by his dentist—and surviving brother, Dr. Pasquale "Patsy" Spilotro.

I learned that Tony often gave the excuse that he had to "go to the dentist" whenever he was called back to Chicago by his bosses in the Outfit, and those same bosses had grown tired of the federal heat he was drawing to their skim operations. I also learned that the Feds suspected him in at least twenty-two murders (maybe Gene Ritchie's?), and dozens of burglaries. His "Hole in the Wall Gang" had stolen most of the jewelry that he and Michael sold in the Gold Rush. On top of all that, he was carrying on an affair with Lefty Rosenthal's wife, Geri. Tony and Michael were told that when they arrived in Chicago, Tony would be made a boss and his brother would become a "made man" in the Mafia. If you've ever seen the movie *Casino*, you know the details. The character "Nicky Santoro," played by Joe Pesci, was based on Tony.

Maybe if I flirted a little harder, Tony would have ended up with me in a suite at Caesar's instead of in an Indiana cornfield grave. Who knows?

It has always amazed me how we women tend to be flirty with guys like Tony or even David "The Big Guy," who end up being not good husband material, while the good guys are right under our noses, so to speak. That was certainly true of my situation at the Hall of Fame Museum, but this was one time when I actually realized it. It was my own brother-in-law who stepped up to the plate in a big way.

At the time I was, as always, still working closely with the Convention Center in directing tourists both to our new museum business and to the Nevada Palace. By now, the Entertainer's Hall of Fame was operating full tilt, and the Tropicana management was looking forward to the increased traffic we promised to bring to their casino with our customers. The only wrinkle in that adventure was Jan's husband Jerry, with whom I butted heads occasionally over business decisions. Jerry seemed to be the typical egotistical know-it-all lawyer, and I became certain of it when I saw his relationship with his brother.

Jan and Jerry had recently invited Jerry's brother Roger to live with them, just as I often did with my brothers. They also gave Roger odd jobs at the Hall, working along with my brother Aubrey, until he could find something permanent. One day at the Hall, I told Jerry that I thought that he had done a nice thing in helping out Roger.

"Well, it was more your sister's idea," Jerry said. Then he laughed and added, "The wacko just got out of the nuthouse and he didn't have any where else to go."

I didn't get what was so funny about mental illness. Some of the babies I helped in my charity work had congenital mental issues, but they were among the most loveable children I worked with. How someone could be so cold and insensitive, especially to a member of his own family, was beyond me. I now made up my mind that Jerry was a complete ass, and I wondered how much longer my sister could bear to be with him. Interestingly, Jerry's brother turned out to be the total opposite of Jerry. Roger was in fact the most caring person I had ever met. He was so kind to Travis, taking him to baseball games, fishing, et cetera. It was great because I wanted Travis to have a good adult male in his life at all times, and David didn't fit the bill because he was rarely in town anymore, was too jealous, and drank too much.

So I tried to help Roger in any way I could, and since Jerry was mean and rude to him, it made me that much more caring—I don't like to see the underdog kicked when he's down. So, in the evening when work was over, I often invited all the boys from work (except Jerry) over to my house, where we would cook and laugh about things that had happened that day. Roger soon got to know my brother Aubrey very well, which was great because he needed friends to build up his confidence after the way his brother treated him.

One day Roger showed up at my place and told me that his asshole brother wanted him to leave his house, but that he had nowhere to go. I felt very sorry for him.

"What happened?" I asked.

"He has been giving me lithium and I can't do anything except sleep. So one day I put it in his OJ and it caused him to fall asleep later that day in court."

I practically laughed my ass off.

"Couldn't have happened to a better guy," I said.

"Well, with Jerry being a trial lawyer, this was not good," Roger said. "I just wanted him to see what it was like. I can't get a good job if I can't wake up."

"Well, you can stay here and sleep on the couch. I'll drop you off in Garden Grove when I go to Los Angeles." Roger and Jerry's mother lived in the Orange County community and I had talked to her recently and learned that she was anxious for Roger to come and stay with her, especially since she had just lost her husband. She thanked me for being such a good friend to Roger and explained to me that Roger's brothers had not been very good to him ever since he had returned from Vietnam—they didn't understand what he had been through. She had three sons, and Roger, a very patriotic Navy man, was the youngest and the only one that had gone to war.

Pretty soon Jerry called me, looking for his brother.

"He's here," I said.

"You shouldn't let him stay there," Jerry said. "He can be dangerous."

"I don't roll that way," I told him. "I think he's a very good soul. I'll drop him off at your mother's on my way to Los Angeles."

"This is none of your business," Jerry said.

"It is now," I replied without hesitation before slamming the phone down.

Jerry didn't like me helping Roger out, but I didn't care. As I've said, I'm not in the habit of listening to other people's opinions anyway. Roger and I became very close. In fact, he became my best friend outside of Jan. I didn't have to hide David from him and he didn't make judgments about me. I told David about Roger and the situation between him and his brother, and David told me that he was proud of me. "You have such a good heart," he said at the time. After a few days I took Roger back to Orange County to be with his mom, but we stayed in touch every day thereafter.

Now with my brother Bob and his family at my LA place and David spending more time in LA, I felt like I had lost my private getaway retreat. Thus I began driving down to Garden Grove to see Roger, one of the few who understood my situation. During this period, Roger, a master heavy equipment operator, was trying to get his government security clearance so that he could work at the military test site in Nevada (the one UFO buffs call "Area 51".) He gave me his room when I arrived (he took the living room sofa), and always made sure it was stocked with things that he thought would help my stress: fruits and snacks, candles and fancy bubble bath stuff in the bathroom. He had even set up a desk so I could make all my phone calls without being disturbed. Roger and his mother were both so kind and loving to me, and Roger was now clearly my very best friend.

"This is always here for you," Roger told me. "No one will bother you here, not even me. You only need to come out of your room if you need something." I could go into this room and sleep if I needed to, and in fact no one did bother me; I found my new retreat. And I made sure I wasn't followed here!

Of course David wanted to know where I was disappearing to when he couldn't reach me at the condo (thank God this was before cell phones came along), but I wouldn't tell him for fear of what might happen. I just told him I needed time to myself and I couldn't find it in Vegas or Brentwood. I didn't tell him about anyone I knew or talked to because he would just call them and have long conversations with them about me. He was a genius at getting people to spill their guts, but I knew he would never be able to get Roger to tell him anything. Not that there was any big mystery about me, but he was obsessed and I felt it could get dangerous. Additionally, I couldn't live with myself if something happened to Roger.

Although he tried, David was unable to get any sympathy from Jan, whom he tried to ply for information on me in numerous phone calls. However, my brother/housemate Bob was always in his corner, pleading David's case to me.

"He loves you more than anything in this world," Bob told me. "And he gives you everything. Why do you fight with him so much?"

With that I unleashed years of pent-up frustration. I don't think my brother knew what hit him:

"You don't understand, Bob," I began. "He's robbing me of myself. I feel like I'm living in a fishbowl. He picks out what I wear, what I eat, where I go. He plans out of my life months ahead of time, and he spying on me—thanks to you. If I mention one person's name he figures out a way to talk to them about me. I can't live this way. I'm tired of fancy dinners, fancy clothes, fancy people. That's his world, but he doesn't want me to have my own world—a place that belongs just to me. And now he's trying to talk me into picking out a fancy military school for Travis. I don't care if that's what other people do! I want him to go to public schools. I want to be involved in my son's life every day. I want to be a real mommy. He wants to groom him for politics and I have never met a politician that I trusted. They're just a pack of smiling dopes. Christ, the wiseguys have more integrity! I feel like politicians are criminals with a free hall pass."

"But David knows what's best for you," Bob attempted to respond.

"I know what's best for me!" I said. "I need some peace of mind and I can't find it in this relationship. I don't like having someone feel they need to live my life for me. I'm not stupid and I'm never going to be someone's puppet, I would rather be dead. I'm a free spirit. I don't care what society thinks of me! They should worry about what I think of them because so far I haven't met anybody that I'm impressed with. I like people that have no ulterior motives for self-gain—and they're pretty hard to find! My sister is the only one who understands my frustrations. And I know David's calling her because she's telling me even though he asked her not to."

End of conversation. I turned and stormed out the door, taking a walk down Barrington with my dog Fannie. That was the last time my brother tried to plead David's case. I think he finally got it.

Now that I was attempting to put more space between David and I, I decided to pursue something just for me, something David would have ridiculed for sure. Since I was a child I was always curious about acting, and people had always told me that I had the looks, not to mention the attitude, for it. So I started taking classes, and soon I was accepted into the Lee Strasberg Institute, the West Coast version of the legendary New York school for actors that specialized in "The Method" style of acting. The idea was to get inside the head of the character you're portraying and try to relate his or her motives to something in your own experience. Strasberg's former students included Marilyn Monroe, Paul Newman, Robert De Niro, Al Pacino, Dustin Hoffman, and countless other acting giants. So I figured I was in pretty good hands. The school was located in West Hollywood, and I had a great time going there and making new friends, although I told them next to nothing about myself or my life in Vegas. It was another escape and a sanctuary that no one knew about.

During this time I met a friend of Santa Monica Dina's named Rudy Deluca, a writer, director and actor who had written for television series such as *The Carol Burnett Show* and had also written or acted in many of Mel Brooks's funniest movies. Rudy and I made each other laugh a lot, which was what I needed and wanted most. Rudy thought I was funny because of my strong southern accent and the crazy expressions (many learned from my daddy) that I would come out with. He wrote many of them down and told me, "I've got to use these. These are priceless." He invited me to his house lots of times to party with his comedian friends such as Sid Caesar, Mel Brooks, Dick Shawn, and John Byner. We would get plastered and laugh for hours. Rudy and I remain friends to this day.

David was pleased about my new acting hobby because it kept me busy, but I never understood how such an intelligent man seemed to have no idea how many handsome young actors I would be meeting in my new hobby. And he definitely was unaware of how I kept busy on the weekends when I didn't need to be in either Las Vegas or LA. On those days I would drive down to see Roger in Orange County. He was the only one I could be honest with without feeling that I was going to be betrayed. Occasionally he would ride to Las Vegas with me if he didn't have to work, and I'd let him stay at my place with me, Aubrey, and Travis, who was still staying with my sister during the week and with me on the weekends. My other brother, Aubrey, stayed at my place full-time and I trusted him to take care of the house for me while I was in LA; he was a real blessing.

Despite spending four or five days a week in LA, I was still responsible for group sales at the Palace. But as sales director you don't spend time at the actual hotel, you just bring in "the bodies" any way you can. I was always busy with my chaotic life, so luckily I could arrange most of the hotel details on the phone when I wasn't in town. My main source of new business was always the Las Vegas Convention Center, and luckily I was the only PR person in town that the Center wanted to work with since I had known them for so long. I called them at least three times a day from wherever I was and made certain that they knew I appreciated all the bodies they sent our way—I would always comp the Center's staff to Tom Jones's show at Caesar's or other showrooms that I was friendly with. I took care of them and they took care of me. Simultaneously, I would always check with the Palace's manager to make sure he had all the information he needed to block out the rooms. I had it down to a science, and everybody seemed happy. Everybody except David, that is.

I quickly found men who were more than happy to date me when David was on the road. I met a guy named Kenny who was an extremely handsome dentist and amateur bodybuilder—just an average nice guy with whom I could have fun after work and share a few laughs. By this time I was sick of cheating politicians and pampered celebrities—people who actually believed their own bullshit. Although David constantly reminded me that I'd never be happy with an average "Joe Blow," it was just another thing he was wrong about. I actually yearned for a friendship that was not so pretentious.

Other than Jan and Roger, I never told anyone about my twisted relationship with David because I was ashamed that I was with a married man and I didn't like telling my business anyway. As one of my daddy's rules said: "information is ammunition." Nonetheless, David found out I was seeing Kenny; he knew all about him and every move I made. This confirmed to me that I had a spy in my circle, and I assumed it had to be my brother Bob, who now spent every day with David when he was in town. This newest "leak" made me feel both vulnerable *and* furious (again). How dare him intrude in my life this way? I now figured out that he thought I was his property. However, I knew in my heart that no one on this earth owned either me or my thoughts.

One day, a very shaken Kenny showed up at my house. In fact, he could hardly speak. After he gathered his composure we began to talk.

"What's the matter?" I asked.

"Why didn't you tell me you're involved with a wiseguy?" he said.

"What are you talking about?"

"I'm talking about everything I own getting blown to smithereens! My truck was stolen, then taken to the desert and destroyed! The police found it twenty miles north of here, burnt to a crisp. And all my stuff that was in it is irreplaceable! The next day I had a call from someone saying 'Take this as your last warning.' It's a warning to stay away from you!"

I was sick with anger; this was an innocent person who was good and pure, who would never hurt anyone—just a real decent human being. I didn't know what to say except that I was sorry and that I would never knowingly put anyone in danger. Needless to say, Kenny never wanted to see me again. David had won. Kenny turned and stormed out and I called David immediately, tearing into him in the worst way. Although he denied having anything to do with the destruction of Kenny's truck, I knew in my heart that he did. We fought about this for the remainder of our time together, but he would never admit it. It was just one more indication that I had to get out of the relationship.

Thirty years later, my own brother Bob admitted that David had asked him to do away with Kenny's truck, which he did. It was my worst fear at the time, but luckily Bob was never pinched for it. Here is how he confessed it to me:

> "I remember that David picked me up one night in yellow Caesar's house car, a Cadillac. He dropped me off at Kenny's house, where I stole the truck and took it out into the desert, and Kaboom! Bye-bye. It worked because the guy never called you again, did he?"

When my friendship with Kenny was stolen from me, things were never the same between David and me, especially with him knowing that I knew about him blowing up Kenny's truck. Every time I had a drink in me I brought it up, but he still always denied it. I know he didn't personally do it but I knew he had it done, and I just couldn't let go of it. Again I felt like he was controlling my life and he had no right to do so.

The last big fight David and I had was a beaut. It was St. Patrick's Day and I was in Brentwood hanging out with my girlfriend, John Jenrette's old pal "Santa Monica Dina," when we decided to go to the "Cock & Bull" for green beer. The place was packed and it didn't take us long to get invited to a huge table of people celebrating this very special Irish holiday. About three hours into laughing, drinking, and meeting new friends, David showed up out of nowhere! He had somehow found out where I was and he immediately began throwing chairs all over this bar, all the while cussing me for being there. I had never seen him in this kind of rage, and I was actually scared to death. I told Dina, "Just go, I'll call you later." She had been laughing, but now turned serious and asked, "What are you going to do?"

"I'll handle him." After Dina took off, I ran out of there, got into my car and left. I was racing down Sunset Boulevard towards Brentwood when I saw David's car right on my bumper. I sped up fast, which made it hard to take those curves on West Sunset. But if I had put on my brakes he would have rear-ended me and maybe killed us both. Somehow he got in front of me and began slowing down until he finally forced me to come to a stop. He jumped out of his car and came running back to me. I rolled the window down and started in on him.

"You crazy bastard!" I yelled. "You're going to kill us both. Don't act like this! I'm going home. You can meet me there and we will talk." He agreed.

Well, when I got home I turned the tables on him.

"How dare you embarrass me like that? I can go wherever I please and talk to anyone I want." I reminded him that *he* was the married one, not me.

"That's what this is all about, you want to punish me?" he asked in disbelief.

"David, if something happens to you, like you die or get killed, where does that leave me?"

"I'll get divorced if that's what you want, and then we can get married," he answered, knocking me for a bit of loop. "It's just a piece of paper anyway, besides, I'll be with you even when I'm dead!"

Now that scared me. I realized this man's obsession had actually increased, if that was even possible. He was definitely not the person I knew and had respected so much. He was brilliant in so many ways and had always been so good to me. What the hell was happening to him? He was calling my sister, my brothers and my friends all the time, spending hours on the phone with them talking about me. Now he was threatening to haunt me from the grave! This was not the superman I knew.

He finally turned on his heels and left my condo, but he kept calling and trying to connive a way for me to have to meet with him. I tried to dodge his calls, but when I couldn't I made up excuses not to be in his presence, hoping to give him time to pull himself together and move on. We talked on the phone, but I didn't even want to be on the phone with him anymore. That's how much he was scaring me.

"I'm not going to let you go out there and ruin your life with some stupid bastard," he said one night. "I know what you need. I'm the only one that can love you."

What? Could he be right? Now I'm beginning to think maybe I *do* have mental problems passing up a guy like this. Most women would kill to have what he was offering me. They would probably even go along willingly with the loss of their independence. In fact, I know many who did. But I stayed true to my vow to keep widening the distance between us. I just concluded that marriage to a person this controlling who was much more worldly than myself would always lead to fights and make for a terrible climate in which to raise children. I guess I was raised differently than most women.

Our phone conversations were getting shorter because I didn't have a lot to say. I didn't want him to know anything that was going on in my life, and I also didn't want or need his opinion (opinions are like assholes, everybody has one). I continued seeing other people although I never mentioned it to David for fear that he'd blow their stuff up like he had Kenny's. And I made certain that my brother the spy didn't know about my dates either. I knew I just needed a bit of time to figure out how to make a clean break of things.

Chapter Six

Transitions

AFTER THE BIG CAR CHASE and fight on Sunset Boulevard, both mine and my family's worlds started to change quickly. First, the Entertainer's Hall of Fame was shuttered. After it had gotten off to such a promising start, the bottom fell out and tourists just stopped coming—they weren't interested. As promised, we returned the celebrities' things to them, and the expensive wax figures deteriorated rather quickly in Jan's garage. All in all, our investors lost some $700,000, and it represented my first business failure in Vegas.

Soon afterwards, my brother Bob told me he was leaving LA and going back to Tennessee. I loved him and was crazy over the baby, but I relished the idea of having my own place back again. Maybe David and I could even get along better—at least be more civil—if I wouldn't feel like every move I made was being reported back to him.

Bob and his family did soon leave and went to stay with our mother back in LaFollette, but it wasn't long before he ended up in trouble and going to prison, leaving his wife and baby alone with my mother. Well, wouldn't you know it, Bob's wife quickly fell in with a new set of friends and began going out all night and taking drugs. This was very hard on my mother because, since she was still working in the same shirt factory she worked in when I was a young child, she worried that when she would go to work her drugged-out tenant/daughter-in-law wouldn't hear baby Robbie, who was now big enough to open doors and wander off.

Not long afterwards, my sister called to tell me that things weren't going well in *her* marriage. Gee, what a shock! My knowledge of how her husband Jerry treated his brother was enough for me, and now Jan opened up about another issue—an issue I could relate to very well. We were still in the formative stages of getting the museum going when Jerry's personality started to change, Jan told me. At the time we needed the whole town's support in order to make a go of it, but Jerry was so jealous of Jan that he didn't want her to attend publicity events and fundraising galas unless he was able to go with her. But his law firm was growing so fast and he was usually needed there. So if he couldn't go, she couldn't go. Now, Jan told me, Jerry's jealousy had gotten worse (just like David's) and she was starting to understand how I had felt being smothered.

We tried to figure out how in the hell we were going to get out of these relationships. As luck would have it, my strategy was made a lot easier when I learned something from my doctor that I knew would make for a clean break-up: I was pregnant!

Wow! Here I go again, another new adventure in life. I had always prayed to God to let me live just long enough to get my son Travis grown, and then "Please, take me to the next world!" Well, I guess God didn't want me so soon because he's allowed me to stick around until now, more than long enough to raise this new baby.

Although second pregnancies go smoother for some women, regrettably that was not the case for me. During that first trimester I didn't feel like my chipper self—I lost weight and looked sickly. The fact that I was hypoglycemic didn't help matters, I'm sure. My physical and emotional changes didn't go unnoticed by those close to me. Travis was not happy about me having a baby because to him it was just something causing his mother pain, while Roger recognized the signs and didn't even have to be told about the reason for them. I remember the morning in Garden Grove when I sat down to breakfast with Roger and planned to let him in on my condition.

"I have something to tell you," I started to explain before he interrupted.

"I know," he said. "You're pregnant."

"How did you know?"

"I heard you throwing up a lot in your room," he explained.

"Well the cat's out of the bag now."

"Let's get married," he blurted out with no hesitation.

As you might imagine, I was not prepared for this possibility. All I could think of was that for years all I wanted to do was simplify my life, yet all it did was continue to get more complicated. Although Roger was my closest friend, and someone I loved dearly, I was still not at a stage in my life where I craved a marriage and all the compromise that goes with it. I was a free spirit in every sense of the word, no doubt having something to do with the way I was raised in the Tennessee hills. The fact was that I was the rarest of women, the kind that doesn't live to be married.

Roger had been so good to Travis and me, although I had no interest in marrying him or anyone else on this earth. I told Roger that I'd have to think this over, but it actually didn't take long for him to get me to see the wisdom of his suggestion. I was desperate for Travis to have an adult male in his life, and I certainly wanted the same for my yet-to-be born child. So I said yes to Roger because of what I thought my children needed more than what I needed or wanted. As a side effect, my marriage would hopefully be the last straw for David, and would put an end to his obsession once and for all.

Before I dropped this latest bomb on David, the pregnancy played a part in my having to cut back on my acting classes, and I would stop altogether after about a year because of one key drawback: my thick East Tennessee accent. Although my coaches told me that I could be a good actress and had commercial looks, they insisted that I had to lose the accent if I hoped to go much farther with it. Thus I attended special speech classes at least three times a week. I was given what I thought were ridiculous vocal exercises that that made me feel like an idiot performing in front of a mirror at home, or on the freeway, driving along while other drivers stared at this crazy woman talking to herself.

But ultimately, the whole attempt came crashing down. My speech therapist, as renowned as he was, couldn't conquer my hillbilly background. I was one of the only failures he ever had. At one of our last sessions he told me, "Franny, you're the only person I know who can take a one syllable word and turn it into three." Oh, well, at least I knew I had acting ability, and looking back, I'm sure it had served me well throughout my crazy life. Soon I would have to hope that talent would convince David of the origins of my pregnancy.

I not only had to tell David I was pregnant, but also that the baby was not his. Oh, and one other thing: I was getting married. I knew it was best to hear this from me rather than anyone else, and I hoped this news might convince him to give up on me. I was certain that he wouldn't hurt me knowing I was pregnant. So I called him and asked when he'd be back in Las

Vegas again because I needed to talk to him. Well, that piqued his interest and he arrived a week later.

We met at the Aladdin, and it was a very emotional "last date" during which we both cried. He was even counting back the weeks and said this baby could be his. But it was just his wishful thinking. The math didn't work and he was smart enough to know it.

"No, David, it's not yours," I tried to convince him. "I know when it happened and it's not your baby, I swear to you."

"I want a name," he said. "Who's the father?"

But I wouldn't give up a name for fear of what he might do. At this time, his friends like John Gotti were still walking the streets. I even worried that he might rope my brother Bob into committing another felony.

"You've got to be kidding?" I said. "After what you did to Kenny?"

Interestingly, this time he didn't deny being behind the destruction of Kenny's property.

"You know how much I love you," he pleaded.

"I know how much you *think* you love me," I said. "But the kind of love that works is not a controlling love like yours. You want me to know how much you love me, but I want you to know how much I need to be a free spirit. It means more to me than anything—except Travis and this new baby."

Somehow I calmed him down and pleaded with him to let me go and have that "white picket fence" life. The look in his eyes told me that he was finally starting to "get it." He asked me if I would continue to work for him, but I told him I didn't think that was possible. And I added that, as much as I liked the condo in Brentwood, it represented his control over me and I wanted to move out as soon as possible. He nodded in understanding.

"We'll always be friends, though, right?" he asked.

"Of course," I answered with tears now running down my face. "You've done so much for me, Travis, and my brother that you are a part of the family."

We hugged and David turned and went out the door.

So once again I packed my Tennessee washboard wedding gift and my closet full of fancy clothes, tossed them into the car David had bought me, and made still another drive up Interstate 15 to Vegas. I would still visit LA on occasion, and when I did I took Rudy DeLuca up on his offer and stayed in his guesthouse.

Roger and I did get married, and, with all the money I had saved working for David, I bought a place that looked like a little dollhouse on the east side of Las Vegas —and, yes, it had a white picket fence. I prepared a nursery for the baby and settled in to growing fat and old. Roger had found a good job in California and only came to Vegas on the weekends, so I stayed at home and took care of myself and Travis. Roger drove home on Friday afternoons and left again on Sunday afternoon, but always made sure I had everything I needed for the week. He hated the long drives but that's where his job took him. And David would still call a couple times a month to see how I was doing. I, of course, always gave him the impression that life was wonderful.

Roger typically walked in the door on Fridays at seven, but he was running a little bit late on the Friday that I went into labor. Thus, my little big man Travis became the stand-in for my new husband, and I taught him to keep time for me when my contractions started. The poor child was a nervous wreck, but he performed beautifully. Roger walked in just in time to call my sister and then take me to the hospital, where Jan was waiting for us.

Labor went by quickly and in about an hour I gave birth to the most beautiful—and healthy—baby girl, Janice Jade (Janice after my sis, and Jade after the name of the Brooke Shields character in "Pretty Baby.") Travis, who had never seen a newborn before, fell in love with Jade, as we called her, as soon as he saw her; he couldn't believe how tiny his new sister was. Giving birth to a girl not only came as a surprise, but one that left me more than a bit anxious because I worried that a girl baby would be more fragile than Travis had been. And, as you might guess by now, Franny Marcum doesn't do "fragile" very well. I was so scared. Of course I called my mother back in Tennessee with the news, but I also wanted her advice.

"Mom, I've had a little girl," I said. "But I have no idea how to take care of a girl."

"You take care of her the same way you took care of Travis," mom advised. And that's exactly what I did. We brought her home and settled in to being a normal family. I remember singing the only lullaby I knew, that crazy "Knoxville Girl," to Jade when I put her down at night. And if you think that's the end of the story you haven't been paying attention very well: my life and the word "normal" were obviously never meant to coexist.

Little Jade was just two months old when Roger didn't arrive on Friday as usual. I heard nothing from him, so I called his mother in Orange County, who also knew nothing—she assumed he was here with us in Las Vegas. Now I was in fear that he had gone off his medication and had an accident on the Interstate. I checked the hospitals and police stations in both Orange County and Las Vegas, but there was nothing reported. I was sick with worry. Roger didn't turn up that night, or the next night, or the next...

This went on for a month with no word to anyone. What could have happened to him? When my mother called to check in one day I didn't want to tell her about my missing new husband, but I broke down on the phone and out it spilled.

"Come home," she begged me. "I don't want you by yourself."

As soon as she said these words it hit me that she was right. I had been longing to get back to the hills that always brought comfort to me. I also had come to the conclusion that Roger had just run off; if he had had an accident I would have been told by now. So I had gone from worried for him to being let down by him—just one more untrustworthy member of the male species, I said to myself. So, before leaving for LaFollette, I filed for divorce from Roger and resolved that I would raise my kids on my own—no more quickie marriages, no more marriages just for the kids' sakes. I would be a single mom and proud of it. Luckily, Nevada is a "no fault" divorce state that requires little more than a low filing fee and, Voila!—you're divorced. And, thanks to my two-time ex, Dan, I was quite familiar with this local regulation.

I bought plane tickets for the three of us, and our brood flew to Tennessee, where mom had little Robbie, and I now had my two. It was crowded but we were all together and having a wonderful time. My mother was thrilled to see her new granddaughter, and I tried to put everything out of my head and just enjoy my mother and the kids. We stayed three weeks before we decided that we wanted to get back home to Vegas. So I headed back west and into a big unknown with two kids, no job, and no man in the house. But I felt invigorated after a few weeks in the country and ready for whatever life brought me. I would need a job soon since my bank account was running low after buying the house, so that would be high on my priority list. I thought I could have probably guessed the kinds of things that lay ahead (in addition to diaper changing): drinks with some old wiseguys, more occasional run-ins with David, a fling or two with a star of one of the Strip showrooms, etc. But there was one adventure I never would have predicted: smuggling illegal aliens.

With still no word from Roger, I settled into the life of a single mother. I was a bit overwhelmed because I was pretty much on my own at this point; Jan, who would have normally been there for me, was likewise entering a new phase of life that prevented her from pitching in. Once the museum folded, Jan began to take up songwriting in her new spare time and was visiting Nashville a lot, making the rounds with producers and record companies. (Believe it or not, my kid sister eventually scored a top ten Billboard hit with her song "Jukebox Junkie" in 1994.) There were periods where she spent weeks on end in the dominion of my dear old friend, Fate Thomas.

After a month back in town, I finally got a call from Roger, and it was very awkward talking to him.

"Are you okay?" I asked with a voice that said I really didn't care.

His big news was that he had been on a fishing trip and had no way to call me. And my news to him was: "Well, you're now a divorced man, so you can fish all you want now." And just like Dan, he asked why I filed so quickly.

"I think of my children first," I answered. "And I will not take on any man's issues. I have no hard feelings for you, and I thank you for the time you were here when I needed you. But I need people in my life I can rely on every day, not just once in a while."

Roger took the news surprisingly well and said that he knew that the marriage probably wouldn't have lasted anyway, due to his Vietnam demons. Our friendship actually endured after the divorce and he stayed in touch, calling regularly to see if the children were OK and if I needed any money. My answer was always the same: "No, I'm just fine." Likewise David would check in at least once a month to see if I needed anything. Same answer. When I told him what happened and that I was now divorced, he gloated, "I told you that you couldn't live with a Joe Blow." In my heart I now wondered if he might be right, but I was not about to turn the clock back and go back to him. On the other hand, I probably *could* live with a "Joe Blow," just not one who disappeared for weeks on end!

After a couple of months, I called a friend of mine who published a tourist guide magazine in town called *What's Up?* He offered me a job handling advertisement sales for the magazine and I quickly accepted. With me knowing the key hotel people this would be an easy job. The problem was I was no longer free to work on my own schedule. In this job I would have to work more or less nine to five out of their office. Luckily, I had met a wonderful lady in the neighborhood who did babysitting in the hotels, so she was licensed and had a health card. I needed this reassurance to feel good about leaving my children with her.

Our publisher was out of the country in Manila most of the time, so it was a relaxed work atmosphere, with no one looking over your shoulder. I worked hard at my new job, and once again my PR skills paid off. It felt good being back out there pressing the flesh, and I doubled the magazine's ad sales in the first week, which meant more money for me also because I received a commission over my salary. Soon the magazine grew into a big business and everybody was happy. I was back to making great money and the kids were doing well with their new living situation.

Back in LaFollette, things weren't going so smoothly for another new mom. My own mother had taken her retirement early in order to stay at home with baby Robbie, and she eventually ended up in court taking full custody and raising him as her own. However, mom was now in her sixties and this was a huge undertaking at her age, so she often sounded completely drained when Jan and I spoke to her on the phone. So, in order to help her out, Jan and I moved her to Las Vegas, where Jan had a guesthouse built on her property in the ranch community known as Spring Valley; it was plenty big enough for both our mother and her newly adopted son. This way mom could also take care of Jan's big house while still having her own home, which was important to her. But more importantly, Jan and I would be there to help her whenever she needed anything. About this time, my boss also needed something, but it was a much bigger undertaking than an occasional ride to the grocery store.

One day my magazine's publisher called me from the Philippines with a request unlike any I had heard before.

"I have something you might be interested in," he began. "I have three girls that work for me here in Manila, but they want to come to the states. I can use two of them to take care of the office, and I'm hoping you can take the other one to help around your house. She will have to live with you, but she can take care of your kids and all your housework too, very cheap. Then it won't be so hard on you."

"Do you know this person well enough for me to take that chance?" I asked.

"Of course," he said. "I would never suggest this unless I knew it would work out for both of you. I can smuggle them out of here and into San Francisco, but you are going to have to take it from there. I'll give you the name and number of the contact in San Francisco, and he'll want a few hundred dollars to get them from there to Las Vegas. Then you will pick them up, take two of them to my house and the one named Lita to your house."

"Do they speak English?" I asked.

"Not very well," he said, "but good enough for you to communicate with them. I'll come in a week or so to take care of my two, but in the meantime all three will need food, money, and transportation until I get there."

Call me crazy, but I agreed to become a human trafficker—for all the right reasons, of course. My boss's contact called when the three arrived successfully in 'Frisco (I have no idea how they got there), and, as promised, I wired $900 to his nearest Western Union office, and the three twenty-somethings soon arrived in Sin City via Greyhound bus. I took them to eat first thing, as I didn't know how long it had been since their last meal—they were so tiny and frail. From there I drove all three girls to my house and introduced them to my children. They were very loving girls and so happy to be in the States. I offered them Travis's room, saying that I would put him on the couch, but they wouldn't do it, and insisted on sleeping on the floor. Of course I made it comfortable for them, and it wasn't long before they were all asleep. I remember standing there, looking at these three very tiny girls as they slept. What have I done? I asked myself. Oh well, God has always looked out for me before and I was sure he would this time too.

I didn't go to work the next day because I wanted to get the girls settled in. I called my boss in Manila and told him, "Mission accomplished. Everybody's happy. I'll see you when you come home." I didn't want to say much on the phone—that was the way I had been trained by David and everybody else I had worked for in this town. As instructed, I took two of them to his place, got them settled in, and then off to the grocery store. It was quite a sight: me, Travis, baby Jade and the three Filipino girls making our way through the store's aisles together. I didn't buy anything beforehand because I didn't know what kind of food they ate, and once we entered the grocery, I just turned them loose and told them to get whatever they wanted. I even made them pick out personal hygiene items I thought they might need; I could tell they were embarrassed but I insisted. I had to know they were comfortable at my boss's house, telling them that I would be back to take them to the office in the morning. It did my heart good to see them so happy and overwhelmed with the good food and accommodations we offered them. It was clear that they had nothing like this in Manila.

Lita, myself, and the kids all went back to my place, where Lita immediately started taking care of both the children and the house. She was wonderful and it didn't take long until she felt like one of the family. When my boss returned from Manila I asked him how much I should pay Lita and he told me to give her fifty dollars a week, which he said would seem like

Lita

a lot to her. But I didn't feel that was enough and I want to be fair to her, so I doubled it.

Lita was with me for a year when I found out that her two other friends had been deported. They had been caught down at the office cleaning after hours and the police were called. I didn't want this to happen to Lita, but I knew she wouldn't be safe here, so close to where her friends were nabbed. So I put my dollhouse up for sale and planned to move away and out into the desert so that no one could track Lita down. She was by now a member of our family and I will protect my family, no matter what it takes. I sold the house very quickly to my neighbors, and actually made a good profit. With that money I leased a small ranch on Tina Lane, about 16 miles north of the city, and not far from Jan's Spring Valley place. I even bought a couple of horses (I had often ridden my neighbor's horse bare-back in Tennessee and had loved horses ever since.)

We all loved the ranch; it gave me a chance to teach my children about animals and Lita a place to hide from the law. We had four horses, a baby goat, a few little chicks and my dog, Fannie—they were all there for Jade and Travis to play with (although Jade never liked the goat, who just kept knocking her over.) Lita took care of the house and I took care of the animals. Every morning, I'd rise while it was still dark (just like my mom had always done) and head into the barns to muck the stalls and feed the horses. Meanwhile Lita rousted the kids, got them fed and had Travis ready for school. I made sure each horse was exercised every day—that meant four separate long rides for me, since I was the only one there able to do it. It all made for a tiresome, long day, but we all loved it and slept like babies every night.

For the first time since leaving LaFollette, I actually felt like I was home, surrounded by loving family members, friends with no agendas, and my loving animals. My kids, who had by now acquired the nicknames "Take Me" (Travis) and "Gimme" (Jade), were happy as jaybirds and loved their new nanny, Lita.

We existed in this paradise for almost two years before an incident took place that shook us to the core. It was an occurrence that not only made the all the local papers and TV news shows, but it also showed me that my tiny daughter "Gimme" was a chip off the old block. The drama began on a typical Friday evening in September 1985, around 6:30 p.m., as I prepared for our ritual weekend recreation known as "cow penning."

This is me at the new ranch

In cow penning, which has been around as a competition since the forties, a team gets 90 seconds to separate three cattle from a herd of about 30 and direct them into a pen at the opposite end of the arena. Whichever team achieves the best time is the winner. The sport requires strong teamwork. With my horseman brother-in-law Jerry on my team, we took my best mare out on Saturday nights for the competitions. Jerry and my sister Jan had been able to breathe a second life into their relationship, but we still had our doubts. In any event, Jerry was nice to me and made a good cow penning partner.

One Friday evening before an event, Jerry had come out to the ranch to load up my mare Alice, a fidgety first-time entry horse, onto his new horse trailer, which was attached to his new truck. However, we were having no success loading the horse— she had a bad habit of biting, especially men and other horses. After Alice tried to bite Jerry he told me, "You're going to have to use another horse. You can't take her to competitions because she's too wild. You need to break her from biting. I'm afraid to put her in with my horse."

While this scene was playing out, two-year-old Jade was walking around us, playing with a kitten that someone had dropped off in front of my house that very morning. I had her dressed like a little cowgirl, in a bright red shirt, new Dingo boots and Levi's jeans.

After a time, Jerry decided to chuck the night's event and try again next week, while we decided on a new horse for that event. While Travis was on the porch waving goodbye to his uncle, Jerry backed out of my driveway and headed back into town and to his house. When he left I looked around to see where Jade was—she was just at the foot of the porch stairs seconds earlier, so I thought she had gone back into the house.

"Travis, go inside and check on your sister," I said. "She's carrying that cat around by its head, and it might scratch her up."

Travis came back out and said, "Mom, she's not in the house."

I thought, she has to be—she was just here beside me. I went inside the house and called out her name because she would usually answer me instantly. I looked under the beds, in the closets, while calling her name more sternly; she was only two years old and so tiny she that could have hidden anywhere. However, I soon realized that she wasn't in the house, so I began to panic. I ran outside still calling for her, while Travis was running around the house screaming also. There was nothing outside our ranch but open desert as far as you could see—deadly open desert.

"Jade, Jade where are you?" we yelled. I called my sister and told her about my missing baby.

"When Jerry gets there have him look in the horse trailer, she might have gotten into it some way."

Next, I called the police, hardly making sense because I was hyperventilating and becoming increasingly panic stricken with every passing second. When I hung up I started running out into the desert, screaming and praying over and over to God, "Please let me find my baby." That's all I could say and think about. Soon the police cars pulled up to my house, so I ran back and told them what she looked like. They asked for a picture, and I gave them one and told them what she was wearing.

In the meantime, more people were driving up to my house. They had also been looking for Jade, although I had no idea how the word had gotten out so fast. Now "search and rescue" was there, and all the hospitals and police in the county were alerted to the situation. I decided that God was the only one I could turn to; I felt he was the only one that could fix this. So I fell to my knees on the desert floor and begged Him, "Please let me find my baby and let her be alive." Just then I heard a banging noise on the porch, and I thought that my prayer was answered. I raced back to the porch to find not Jade, but poor little twelve-year-old Travis, who was pounding his head against the wall and crying loudly for his beloved little sis. I ran over to him, grabbed him and held him tightly as we both collapsed into each other's arms. I told him, "We have to pray to God. He's the only one that can help us."

In the house the phone rang, and my mind raced with both dreaded fear and hope. It was my sister calling me back with terrible news: Jerry had arrived home, and the answer was no, Jade was not in the horse trailer. My only hope had now vanished. I now knew where Jade had to be. So again I started running through the desert, screaming her name and praying. I will never forget how my heart felt, knowing that grown men didn't last long in that harsh environment. I would be lying if I said I didn't picture her being ravaged by coyotes. That memory is still so fresh that it makes this event so difficult to even write about all these years later. But this story has to be told.

This hell went on for two to three hours, and I was beginning to feel as though all my strength and energy had been drained from my body when the phone rang. It was Sunrise Hospital. They told me they had a "Jane Doe" there that fit the description of the little girl that was missing.

"Is she all right?" I asked in desperation. But whoever was calling either didn't know the child's condition or wasn't allowed to tell me anything. They just wanted to know if I could come down to the hospital to make an identification. *An identification?* I cannot explain how I felt. At times it seemed like numbness, and a minute later like the onset of a nervous breakdown. I was praying it was Jade, but at the same time I was scared to death of what I might be facing.

A neighbor girl who was at my house helping in the search offered to drive me the seventeen miles or so into town (mostly on what were then dirt roads.) I jumped into her truck with my heart beating so fast that I could hardly breathe. That 45-minute drive to the hospital felt like an eternity. And just when things couldn't get more horribly surreal, they did.

About five miles from the hospital, the girl's car ran out of gas at a red light. I was now about to pass out from nervous exhaustion when we noticed a gas station that just happened to be on the very corner where we came to a stop. We jumped out of the truck and pushed it to the station with the help of people stuck behind us. Then I realized that I had no purse with me—in all the excitement I had left home with nothing. Likewise, the girl who owned the truck had no money on her.

"Oh, my God, please do something," I cried out loud. I grabbed the attendant and begged him to trust me. I explained where I was going and what had happened to my baby. I must have scared the poor man half to death with the emotional state I was in, but he gave me the gas and away we went. I arrived at the hospital only to see the media all over the place, but I shoved my way through, and when I got to the main desk I explained who I was and why I was there. They proceeded to ask me for identification, but I didn't have any because, again, I didn't have my purse. I explained this but the receptionist still refused to tell me anything, not even where to go. I was getting louder and louder—this woman had no idea how close she was coming to having a day in her life that she would never forget. Nothing or nobody was going to keep me from going to see if this "Jane Doe" was Jade.

Of course the police were trying to settle me down, but that wasn't going to work with me. Now every ounce of my Tennessee temper was about to come to the surface. I was within an inch of making that shambles of a bar I destroyed on

Industrial years ago look like something out of *Better Homes and Gardens* compared to what this place would look like if they gave me any more problems.

"I'm going back there to see if that's my baby," I warned. "And you will have a fight on your hands if you try to stop me." Since the media was listening to this I had to be careful not to threaten anyone's life, but I most certainly would have had we have been alone. And it wouldn't have been a bluff.

While I'm arguing with these people, the female hospital administrator came down and said, "Let her go." This lady then took me straight back to the emergency room where they were keeping "Jane Doe." There, on a hospital gurney with all her little limbs strapped down, I saw her. It was my dear baby Jade! She was alive and bruised, but nothing was broken. Words cannot tell you how I felt. All I knew was that God had answered my prayers. After all the hugs and kisses I gave her, I looked up, and there stood Jan and Jerry crying so hard. We were all consumed with emotion. That's when Jade looked up at her uncle and said something that brought chills to the room.

"Uncle Jerry, you hurt me!" This was not good because the police were already asking questions of Jerry. But none of us, including Jerry, had any idea what had happened. We all looked back at Jade.

"What, baby, what happened?" She started to sob and just said, "Where's kitty?"

What the police learned in their investigation was positively hair-raising, and a miracle by the definition of everyone who's heard the details. We learned of it from the man who had found Jade and called the police. I was filled in as the doctors were examining Jade.

Jade had been petting her kitten, when she sat down on a tiny running board behind the wheel-well of Jerry's trailer—on the other side from where we were all standing. When Jerry pulled off she was still sitting there as Travis and I turned to walk back into the house. Almost impossibly,

The arrow is pointing to the little running board where Jade and her kitten were riding

that tiny child and her new pet sat there for almost three miles, despite the bumps in the dirt road. Then it became even more terrifying as Jerry, who had no idea that he was carting Jade and her kitten on the bumper of his trailer, left the ranching community and headed onto Interstate 95, where he would be driving over sixty-miles-per-hour.

As Jerry approached the entrance ramp, Jade and her cat tumbled off and on to the side of the road. As luck would have it, there was an eighteen-wheeler behind Jerry as he made the turn-off. The truck driver later told police that he had to slow down when Jerry made his turn off to the right, and he happened to look through his side view mirror when he noticed something red on the ground. At first he thought the object was a red rag, but he then saw it moving, so he decided to turn around and go back. There he found my little angel lying in the road, clutching the kitten by its neck. He immediately called 911 and stayed with her until the ambulance arrived. He said that when the cat got loose it ran so fast he couldn't catch it, especially while holding the baby. It was never to be seen ever again. But I think that cat must have cushioned Jade's fall.

This was mind boggling to us: how did she stay on this tiny area that was about one-foot square and had nothing for her to hold on to? I also know how a horse trailer bounces around on the road—so why didn't she bounce off when they hit the first bump? What would have happened if someone had not dropped off a kitten that morning, the one that broke her fall? And what if that trucker had not been there at the time? Jade had only two directions she could have walked: back out into the desert, never to be found, or onto the highway.

When they told me I could get her dressed to take her home, it was the happiest moment I could ever remember. I picked up Jade's brand new boots and noticed that the wooden heels were completely gone: she had dragged them all the way to the highway. Again I thought to myself, there's no possible way she could have done this without falling off. I had to ask her.

"Jade, how did you stay on the horse trailer?" She looked up at me and said, "Jesus held me on."

I was speechless–not because I didn't believe in miracles, but because this little child had never heard of Jesus! We weren't churchgoers or Bible readers. So I asked again, thinking perhaps I didn't hear her right or didn't understand her. After all, she's only two years old. But she said it to me again very plain and even more forcefully, "Jesus held me on!" To this day, I take what she said into my heart and mind, and I believe it, because that's the only possible way she could have survived that ride.

The story of Jade's ride was written up in the *Las Vegas Review-Journal* with the headline: **TOT MIRACULOUSLY SURVIVES INCIDENT.** And it was a miracle—it was God answering my prayers with a miracle I will never forget.

But Jade's "terrible twos" had one more punch to throw at us, and this one was even more blood-curdling than the horse trailer incident. A few months after Jade's wild ride, a neighboring rancher was visiting with his family dog, a huge thirteen-year-old Doberman. As Jade and this neighbor's young daughter sat munching snacks in front of the television while the adults chatted in the kitchen, this dog decided to tear into my sweet, *and tiny*, two-year-old, perhaps from a bout of food aggression; Jade later told me that they were totally ignoring the dog when the attack began, while Travis remembers that Jade was playing with the animal, as a toddler will often do, who was trying to sleep. In any case, we heard her horrible screams and raced from the kitchen to find this beast had bitten Jade in the face and left behind two huge puncture wounds that were more like gouges. That's when I grabbed my trusty Remington Fieldmaster 22-gauge rifle from the top of the armoire and unloaded it point-blank into that monster's skull. To me it didn't matter whose fault it was; no animal attacks my kids and lives to bark about it.

Jade was now covered in blood that gushed from deep gashes in her face, including one that ran from the inside corner of her eye, near the tear duct, right down along her nose line. Once more it was a race to the hospital—this time I checked my gas gauge first. To make a long story short, that poor child endured five plastic surgeries over the next nine years before we were done. I used the same plastic surgeon that my friend, and wax museum honoree, Ann-Margret had used to fix a scar on her face. He did an amazing job, and today you would never guess that anything had happened to her.

Ranch life had seemed to be the perfect answer just a couple of years ago, but with all of Jade's misfortunes and Travis needing to find a good high school to enter, I began to consider still another move, this one closer to town. One of the things that sealed my decision was Lita, who was a key reason for moving here in the first place. Lately she was getting more and more paranoid about being found by the authorities—so much so that she wouldn't even go shopping with me. Consequently she stayed in the house during the day doing housework while I took care of the outside ranch chores. Around this time, my younger brother Donnie, who was in the army, was given his first furlough and decided he would stay with me at the ranch for a few weeks. Lita thought he was so rich and good-looking, so she always gave him extra attention. That led me to thinking that maybe I could fix Lita's immigration problem. I approached Donnie with the idea that he could marry Lita, but he wasn't too thrilled about it.

"Oh, no, Black Cat, I'm not doing that," he said. But I bugged him every day with the idea until finally he agreed.

"But, just as long as she understands, there will be no romance in this situation," he insisted. I told him I'd make sure she understood. But when I mentioned it to Lita, it was clear that she was so love-struck that it would be too awkward for all involved, so I dropped the idea, much to Donnie's relief. Of course, Lita was quite sad that the marriage was cancelled.

When Donnie's furlough was over, he packed up to leave and told Lita that he would write her, but he never did. The last straw for dear Lita was when I talked about selling the ranch and moving back closer to town. I told her that I needed to go back to work, and needed to move closer to where schools and jobs were located. I would also be closer to my sister and mom, who could take care of Jade while I worked.

I sold my horses and gave away the other animals. Lita, who had some friends in California, decided to move there. I think she not only wanted to feel safe, but she also needed to get away from things that reminded her of Donnie, whom she had really fallen hard for. We kept in touch for a few years, but eventually lost contact when she finally found someone and got married.

I packed up my kids (and my Tennessee washboard) and moved back into town, where I went to work selling advertising for an equestrian themed newspaper called *Horse Talk*. This was the first year the rodeo came to Las Vegas, a big deal for the city because it was scheduled for December, which was always a slow time for tourism. I buried myself in my work and caring for my two kids. David would still call every once in a while and we would laugh and reminisce about the days of excitement we shared. We stayed friends until the day he passed. I have always felt that, in a way, he raised me because he taught me so much.

In 1986, not long after returning to Vegas, the kids and I attended Jan and Jerry's annual Thanksgiving dinner at their place, where our mom was still living. Of course, Roger (my ex and Jerry's brother) was also there, but since we remained friends, it wasn't all that awkward. At some point in the get-together I mentioned how I needed to get health insurance for my family, but was worried about coming up with premium payments. Roger said that his new job not only provided family insurance, but paid so well that he was in need of some tax write-offs—like kids, for example.

With the wine flowing after the kids were down, one of us suggested the crazy idea of getting remarried, at least for financial reasons. It was an idea that I was well acquainted with, of course. Well, long story short, we got hitched again and moved down to Roger's home in Garden Grove. Since Roger was still a dear friend (despite his month-long disappearance that led to our first breakup) our remarriage began to feel like a normal marriage. It was what Jade refers to as the closest we ever came to a "June Cleaver, white picket fence" life, with frequent family trips to nearby Disneyland and Pacific beaches. Of course, with me not being the romantic kind, I always had one foot out the door, no matter how well things were going. I would always be hopelessly independent; it's in my blood. So, just when we seemed all settled, two things happened in rapid succession that forced my other foot out of June Cleaverland.

First up was the October 1987 Whittier earthquake, which hit us at 7:40 a.m. I had never experienced anything like this, and was rattled to my core when everything on our shelves came crashing down and breaking into a million little pieces. Right then I seriously considered moving out and heading back to Las Vegas. But I stayed on. Then about a month later I found out that Roger was in deep trouble with the IRS. I now concluded that his desire to use my kids as tax write-offs was linked to some bigger problems with the feds. I felt that he had hidden something from me that he had no right to, and his admission led to a huge fight. A week later I packed up four-year-old Jade and headed back to Vegas. I told Roger, "I'm going to Vegas for a couple of days to cool off." But I ended up doing exactly what he did to me in our first marriage: I stayed away for thirty days, only to return to Garden Grove to tell

Roger "It's over." Soon I signed papers for my fourth divorce to only two different husbands. Crazy.

Sixteen-year-old Travis stayed behind with Roger because he was enrolled in Garden Grove High School, had friends there, and, frankly was exhausted from all the moves. In Vegas, I was a single mom—again! I doted over little Jade, but I worked hard to teach her right and wrong. My kids would tell you that I was a strict single mom; I didn't have a lot of rules, but God forbid if you broke one. I still believe that a quick dose of corporal punishment is a good thing, even if it's no longer politically correct. It was a part of my upbringing that I inherited and actually agreed with—although obviously not to the extent that my father employed it when he was drunk. Both Jade and Travis remember one of my expressions very clearly: "Go pick out a switch. And if you come back with a twig, I'll go pick one out that you'll really regret."

Sometimes there was just no twig available, like the time I punched 16-year-old Travis square in the kisser when he disrespected me in the grocery store. The boy went flying into the frozen turkey bin and was on his back and covered frozen turkeys. He was out of it for a couple of minutes, and he reminded me of when I had seen Thomas "Hitman" Hearns on the canvas at Caesar's in 1985. The other shoppers were shocked when I just turned on my heels and continued shopping. When Jade became a teenager and mouthed off, she got a similar treatment, including once in the same store. In that instance I bashed her in the face with a bag of raw, bleeding meat parts. Again, shoppers were horrified, this time at the site of a pretty teenage girl covered in blood—they didn't know it wasn't hers.

Then there was my other side…

I still did charity work whenever I found time. In fact, that's how I met my present husband. The Arthritis Foundation had approached me about working for them, heading up all the their fundraisers. I agreed and received a good salary for doing something I knew about and enjoyed. One of the events they wanted me to coordinate was a benefit golf tournament. The director said to me, "You don't need to know anything about golf. We need someone to donate a golf course for the day and seventy-two golfers willing to pay to play in this event." Well, I knew nothing about golf at that time, but I was fully capable of wrangling enough players to make this a success, which it was.

The day of the tournament was my first time on a golf course—I had to be there to meet and greet all the players I had recruited for the cause. The golfers were set to have a fun day, with donated prizes going to the winners. About two hours into the tournament my boss called for me.

"I have an idea," he said. "You take a golf cart, go around to each golfer, and if they make a shot they don't like, tell them you will let them have a Mulligan for five dollars, so any bad shot won't go against their score."

This made no sense to me because I knew nothing about golf. But since it would raise more money for the foundation I was happy to do it. So I asked the director to explain the concept again.

"A Mulligan is when you get to do your shot over if you don't like it," he explained. "Some call it a 'do-over.' Golfers know what this is, but you're going to charge them for doing it. Here's a roll of raffle tickets. When they buy a Mulligan they can put their tickets into a raffle bowl to win a prize." Now I got it, and off I went in my cart.

The first team I stopped was three guys on the tenth putting green—that much I understood. I pulled up, got out of the cart, and noticed that these guys were having a hard time making putts. I decided that they might need my do-over deal, but my brain froze, and for the life of me, I couldn't remember the word for it. The word "over" was the only thing churning around in my brain. When I opened my mouth it just came out all wrong, and reminded me of when I bragged about owning a hernia when I was fourteen years old.

"Do you guys want to buy some of my over-ies?" I yelled out.

Well, these guys froze in place, then looked at me like I was nuts. So I explained.

"When you don't like your shot you pay me five dollars and you can do it 'over,'" I said as I watched them start to howl in laughter just the way my brother and his young wife did all those years ago.

"You mean a Mulligan?" they said in unison.

"Yeah, that's the word," I answered.

These guys were now cracking up uncontrollably but I really had no idea why. One guy in the group gathered himself and spoke up.

"Stay right there," he said, as he came over, introduced himself as Chuck, and bought nine Mulligans from me—three each for him and his partners. Well, this Chuck, the guy I sold the forty-five dollars in "ovaries"

(L-R) Chuck, Me, and Dan Poole

to, ended up becoming my husband! Chuck and I dated for a year before he popped the question. He was different than any other guys I had dated, straight up and honest. He was even totally different from me: he came from a religious background and was raised by a very loving family. He had been given all the things I had not, but always wished for. I've always heard that opposites attract, and in our case it was true. I knew this was exactly what I needed and wanted. I had enough excitement in my life. We married when Jade was six years old. By this time, Travis was just out of high school, and he moved in with his girlfriend at her family's home.

Chuck owned a successful insurance company and he convinced me to get my license, which I did, although I took a job with another company because I don't think that living together and working together is a good idea for any relationship. Chuck turned out be the low-key, honest man I had always looked for, but until now I could never find. And I became an avid golfer to boot!

Meanwhile Jade was growing into a stunning looking little girl with a strong interest in acting. For years we watched her "putting on shows" in Jan's barn, then we were amazed when, with absolutely no experience, she landed the lead role in the recreation center's production of *Alice in Wonderland*. After this, she really got the acting bug, and it has never left her. At fourteen she auditioned for the Las Vegas Performing Arts Academy, passing an audition before a nine-member panel of judges. The magnet school was opened in 1993, with 700 students who "majored" in some aspect of the performing arts. It was a strict academic school where Jade excelled as (what else) a theater major. However, there was a downside to this place—it was crammed with spoiled little divas who had been groomed since they were toddlers to be celebrities. Their oversized egos just couldn't handle it when Jade not only landed great roles in the school's productions, but also got signed to a modeling contract by the *John Robert Powers Agency* during her freshmen year. This company boasted alumni such as Grace Kelly, Jackie Kennedy, Ann Margret, Raquel Welch, Lucille Ball, Gene Tierney, Tyrone Powers, Jennifer Jones, Marlene Dietrich, Ava Gardner, Cary Grant, and many more.

She soon fell prey to the Academy's "mean girls" who bullied her relentlessly, and their methods included beating the poor girl up. To this day I am certain that jealousy was behind much of it because Jade had grown into an intelligent, beautiful young girl, with looks that most of her classmates would kill for, and an acting ability that came effortlessly to her. This is when I learned where Jade and I were different; when someone started something with me in school (believe me, it wasn't very often), I would tear into them ferociously (boy or girl) until somebody pulled me off. Jade, on the other hand, internalized all the wounds and just seethed inside. As often happens with these victims, Jade entered into her own dark world, which for her meant adopting the "Goth" look long before it was fashionable. She also began to show an interest in serial killers, and was excited to do a school report on axe murderer Lizzie Borden. (I sure hope that my nightly singing of "Knoxville Girl" to her as a lullaby when she was a baby didn't have anything to do with this, but I suppose it could have.)

Jade's new style only made the bullying that much worse. When she came home from school one day all bruised from a horrible beating, I raced down to the Academy and into the principal's office, demanding to know the name and address of the parents of the girl. Luckily for all involved, the principal refused to give me those details, but he apologized and the next day called to say that the girl who hurt Jade had been sent off to another school, but it was already too little too late for us. Earlier that morning, Jade came to me with a look in her eyes that I had never seen before.

"Please, let me be home-schooled," she practically begged me.

She didn't have to ask twice. That very day, after hanging up on the Academy principal, I was down at the local library where I learned about various home school associations that would guide me through the process in exchange for a tuition fee and $517 dollars for Jade's first year of textbooks. Now the craziest part of all this was that I was a high school dropout (I never told Jade this) who now had to teach my daughter things I had never learned in order to help her get a diploma.

For the next two years, while the Powers Agency lined up auditions for Jade, I was up late at night learning things like algebra and chemistry so I could teach it to her the next day. From that point on, we were down at that library once a week so she could take her tests. I must have done a good job because she got her diploma (not a GED!) at 16. This was a year too late for her to accept a contract that was offered to her to be in the TV series *The Gilmore Girls*—the Screen Actors Guild wouldn't allow her to sign without her diploma. My tutoring had only been interrupted by a family drama that would lead to what I hope will be my final whirlwind adventure.

About one year after Chuck and I married, my kid brother Donnie, a security agent at the Stardust, was transferred to a new casino in Jackson, Mississippi, where he would be in charge of all security. It was a great promotion for him, and he deserved it—he had just come off of a horrible marriage, and had two children to support. To all of our shock, Donnie's ex, Maryann, had convinced him to get back together, and she was waiting with him at his house when I came to take him—now *them*—to the airport. I was pissed, and I knew this great opportunity would end badly.

Well, as expected, Donnie called me a year later—from a Mississippi jail! He had been arrested and convicted for shooting Maryann after he caught her cheating on him while their kids were locked in their room. He told me that he was in a horrific jail in Philadelphia, Mississippi, and looking at 25 years in prison if somebody didn't do something fast—his sentencing was in two weeks. I had to get involved; my baby brother was a good man who just got mixed up with a bad woman. I told him I would come down and try to figure something out. I then called up my brother JR's wife Carol in Atlanta and she agreed to go with me to Mississippi to get to the bottom of this mess.

Now I knew something about small Southern towns, but Philadelphia was about as stereotypical as you could get, full of racist good ol' boys who hated outsiders and pretty much shot them at will. The town was made infamous in 1964 when three young civil rights workers were murdered there, with not a whit of legal action on their case for over forty years. I knew we were up against it, but I had to try to help Donnie.

As soon as we arrived in Philadelphia, we could tell this hick town never heard the expression "Southern hospitality." After checking in at the town's only motel, Carol and I were not only shunned by everyone we tried to talk to, but the local cops followed us everywhere we went. We assumed (correctly) that Maryann had put the word out about us. After three days of leaving huge tips in the restaurant where we ate every day and going out of our way to compliment the cook and waiters, we finally got a break when the female restaurant owner asked me to speak with her outside.

"Are you Donnie's sister?" she asked in hushed tones out behind the dumpster. After I answered yes, she told me that she could tell that Carol and I were good people and that she'd give us some information if we kept her name out of it. I gave her my word.

"Maryann has told everyone that your family is connected to the mob in Vegas," she told me. "That's why the cops are following you and why no one will speak to you." I swore to her on my kids' lives that we had nothing to do with the mob, we just wanted to see that Donnie was treated fairly. Well, this woman took a shine to me and told me something that changed everything for Donnie.

"His wife is not only a whore," she said, "but among the many men she's screwed is the very judge who presided over your brother's trial—the same one who's going to sentence him next week." After she told us where the bitch worked, I started for the car. I was going to finish what Donnie had started. Before I could get in the car, Carol grabbed my arm and stopped me.

"You're too hot, Franny," she said. "Just cool down for a minute. Maybe we can come up with a plan that will help Donnie. I know that beating Maryann into the ground won't do him any good."

She was right. We decided that I should go to Maryann's place of work, put on the charm, and apologize profusely for my brother's actions. I did just that, and over the next four days I treated Maryann to the most expensive meals I could find in this backwoods burg. I soon got the feeling that I was her new best friend as the "girl talk" started flowing; she had no idea that I still hated her guts and was only using her to get dirt on the judge. Late on the fourth night, after we had emptied a bottle of red wine, she spilled the beans.

"Want to know something funny?" she asked.

I sure did.

"This judge, who's married by the way, is the biggest hypocrite of them all."

How so?

"He cheats on his wife all time." (Pause) "I should know."

I'm all ears.

"He's got this houseboat that he keeps down on Okatibbee Lake. He only has it so that he can take girls there. Believe me, I know," she laughed as she raised her eyebrows.

Oh, details, please.

"After Donnie and I broke up when he shot me, I spent a night or two there myself. I could barely keep my mouth shut when he was assigned to Donnie's trial. I was so full of hatred for Donnie at the time, but since then I realized that I've been pushing his buttons for years. He just snapped. He was a good husband and he worships our kids."

Check, please.

When the day of the sentencing came around I made certain I was there an hour early—I just wanted to have a friendly down-home chat with the good judge. I spent most of the morning doing my hair, makeup and wardrobe. I looked as good as I ever have just to see if this Hillbilly hypocrite would make a pass at me. All that effort came in handy when I flirted my way past the bailiff so that I could have a few moments alone with the judge in his chambers.

"Yes, Miss Marcum, what can I do for you?" the judge asked from behind his desk, as he eyed me up and down like a three-scoop chocolate sundae.

"I just wanted to let you know how sorry we all are about this thing," I said. "I apologized to Maryann and told her we want to do anything we can to make it up to her."

"I'm sure she appreciates that, but you understand that this has no bearing on your brother's sentencing?"

"Oh, of course. We just wanted you to know."

With that, I got up and turned to the door, then stopped, turned back to him, put my hand to my forehead and tried to replicate that scene that I saw in every episode of *Columbo*.

"Oh, there's just one more thing," I said. "I can't figure out why Maryann wanted to tell me about her nights on some houseboat on Okatibbee Lake. You wouldn't have any idea what that's about by any chance?"

The judge, of course, froze up. Only his jaw moved—it dropped. After a long pause he spoke up.

"Miss Marcum, nothing personal, but I hope I never see you again."

"Judge," I replied as I headed out the door. "Nothing personal against you either, but I feel the exact same way."

A few minutes later we were in the courtroom, where the judge shot me a look before he gave Donnie the lowest possible sentence, four years, of which he only served a year and a half. You gotta love small towns.

Chapter Seven

Postscript

FINALLY, I WAS IN NEVADA and going about the business of leading a more normal life than I ever imagined I was capable of. I owe a lot of that to my final husband Chuck, who combines everything I had looked for in a man: handsome, honest, and easygoing enough to not only put up with me, but to mellow me out and make me a good life partner. I guess time not only heals all wounds, but wounds all heels (an old joke I just had to throw in here somewhere.)

In 2001, I began fostering two sweet little sisters ages seven and five, and last year Chuck and I legally adopted them. So now we are sixty-something chauffeurs, and loving every minute of it. And with Travis's two kids at my house every day there's never a boring moment. Travis, by the way, went on to become a successful tile-setter, got married and had two lovely children of his own. In his spare time, he pursues his passion for music and is the lead singer in a band based in Las Vegas. Today he lives right next door to me, and, as I said, his kids are at my house every day.

As far as the rest of my family goes, I couldn't be more proud. In the nineties I rented an apartment for Jade and I in Laguna Beach so she could go on auditions. Soon after Jade received her high school diploma, she landed the contract role of

"Jessica Bennett" on the NBC soap opera *Passions*, making her a permanent Los Angeles resident.

After spending three years under contract, Jade left to pursue a film career. She has since starred in several indie films, in addition to making a number of television guest appearances. She is currently starring in the Emmy nominated independent serial drama "The Bay," where she plays the drug addicted teenager "Lianna Ramos," and three more of her are projects are slated for theatrical release in 2013.

My beautiful sister Jan finally got divorced from Jerry. I knew Jan too well to believe that she could live with Jerry forever, especially since the two of them were rarely together anymore. They just weren't a perfect match from the get-go. And by this time Jan's successful songwriting career put her in Nashville for weeks on end, while Jerry was also gone most of the time, on the road with his cutting horse events. His law firm had grown big enough by now that he was the senior partner and could afford buying and selling these very expensive horses, and competing in rodeos with them (eventually he would actually become World Champion.) It was obvious that he and my sister were going in two different directions, making lots of money and spending most of their time away from their big house in Las Vegas, where my mother now held everything together. Mom often told me, "They are not together enough anymore. This is what money can do!"

Jan eventually became the first Marcum to receive a college degree (in psychology) just before she and Jerry divorced. As her songwriting career began to take off, she met former Stardust owner Allan D. "Al" Sachs, who was quite a bit older, but well liked by everyone who knew him. Although Jan didn't know it at the time, Al had his own colorful history looking the other way while the Chicago Outfit looted the lost wagers (called "the skim") from the count rooms of his casinos. Al was born on July 17, 1925 in Chicago, where his father was a courier for Al Capone, and got his own casino start as a stickman at the Outfit-controlled Big Game Casino and the Jockey Club. He moved to Las Vegas in 1952 before opening the Royal Nevada Casino three years later.

In rapid succession Al bought the Fremont, became a minor investor in the Tropicana, managed the casino at the Aladdin, and, with mob-connected Vegas icon Moe Dalitz, opened the Sundance. Al, whom the newspapers called "sharp-dressing and easy-going," purchased the Stardust in 1979, where he was known as the go-to casino operator for Chicago wiseguys who traveled to Vegas and who needed

Al Sachs

to be taken care of. I should know—I escorted a few of them from the airport to their suites at the Stardust long before we actually met Al. However, five years after buying the Stardust, Al lost his license and was fined $3 million for not stopping the skim operations in his casino.

Soon after Jan and Al married, Al was diagnosed, first with Parkinson's Disease, then with lung cancer. While being treated in LA, he stayed with Jade in her tiny Sherman Oaks apartment for months, but died of a heart attack in March 2002 at age 77.

"He was always grateful to have lived in a time when, as a young man with no credit, he could talk to the Las Vegas bankers, who would take a liking to him and give him the loans needed to buy the casinos," Jan said. "You cannot do that in today's Las Vegas."

Looking back, it's amazing how Jan's and my lives paralleled each other's beat for beat: our moves to Vegas, our marriages to a pair of brothers, our breakups, divorces—they all seemed to happen simultaneously. Until recently, we were also both always totally identified with the men in our lives, something we had both sworn would never happen when we lived in Tennessee. We had come such a long way, but all the money still didn't make us happy because our men dictated most of the terms. But we finally broke free of that stereotype and made our own marks on the world. Today Janice Sachs works as a program director for an organization that serves developmentally disabled adults in Vegas.

Three years after Al's passing, our mom, the dear Edna Stanford Marcum, lost her battle with Alzheimer's at age 88. She was one tough, but loving lady. After rearing her own brood of seven against all odds in Appalachia (five of whom are still here: JR, Bob, Aubrey, Jan, and me), she raised three of her children's children later in life. I like to think I inherited some of her giving spirit. Her last breath came just four days after I stole her out the assisted living facility where she lived (I told her nurses that I was just taking her outside in her wheelchair to get her some air.) It turned out to be a good thing since in those last days she was surrounded by her kids and grandkids. I slept with her around the clock, and she died in my arms. It was the least I could do, but, sadly, it was all I could do.

And what about David, "The Big Guy"? My dear Svengali/mentor passed on in 2007, at age 73. It was only after his death that I learned details about his life that he never told me, and that I (of course) never asked about. David had been born in Brooklyn, NY on June 13, 1933. After graduating from Georgetown University he began establishing various careers in the hotel, advertising, political, public relations, entertainment and automobile industries. His business career started with executive positions at the Eden Roc, Deauville, and Diplomat Hotels in Miami Beach, before moving back to New York where he got into the public relations game. That's what led to his associations with Shirley MacLaine, Tom Jones and Engelbert Humperdinck.

While in New York, David was heavily involved in Democratic Party politics, eventually becoming director of New York's Democratic state headquarters. He quickly moved up the party ladder, working on both the local and national levels. He served as assistant to the New York Speaker of the House Stanley Steingut and special advisor and advance specialist to Governors Hugh Carey and Mario Cuomo. He served as an advance man for every Democratic presidential campaign from JFK (1960) to Jimmy Carter (1980). These were the years when he became very close to the Kennedy clan.

In 1991, years after we parted ways, David and his wife actually moved to Las Vegas, where he became involved in fundraising for various charities such as Reach Out for Children with HIV & Aids, the Las Vegas Economic Opportunity Board, and Child Haven. He also became the vice president of the Red Rock Democratic Club.

WELL, DEAR READER, THAT'S ABOUT IT. I'm typing these last words, like I did all the rest, from the patio of the lakeside home I share with Chuck and our kids and pets in Lake Tahoe. When I'm not golfing, chauffeuring, or having my daily phone chats with Jan, Jade and Travis, I try to find a minute to catch a little Oprah on the boob tube. It's pretty much the only TV time I give myself. And it's never about her guests on the show—I don't remember (or care about) any of them. It's about her. I identify with her as another single woman from poor Southern roots who cares about children.

I take pride in reading people—in fact, I feel that's my only real talent. I watch Oprah's expressions every day, looking into her eyes, and wondering if she ever thinks about how her life went from A to Z. I know I've thought it about myself. Many times I've wondered: how did I get here? I believe now after watching her all these years that Oprah is a modern day American version of Mother Teresa, giving so much to so many people. I also believe the book of our lives is already written and we are just the actors.

I know Oprah played her role well, and I hope you and I do too.

THE END

Acknowledgements

I would first like to thank all of the people mentioned in this book, each of whom played a role in making me who I am, and for that I am grateful. Of course, special thanks go to my family: my dear mother and father, James and Edna Marcum, who have passed on, but are always in my heart; my siblings, Ralph, James, Aubrey, Bob, and David, and my one and only sister (and partner in crime for so many of these crazy adventures) Janice, who is so much more than a sister to me. We are a pair of survivors who couldn't have done it without each other. Love ya, sis. My husband of twenty-three years, Charles Jensen, has loved and supported me in all my endeavors. He is my hero. My children, Jade, Travis, Ki-eshia, Alicia, and my grandsons, Boris and Cameron Comer: you make my life full. If you read this book, I hope you will understand why your mom/grandmom is the way she is, and most importantly, how much she loves you—and you'd better learn from her mistakes!

When dear Ruthi Greer convinced me to finally share my crazy stories with the world and volunteered to publish this book, the first person to step up was my pal Antoinette Giancana (the real "Mafia Princess"). Knowing that I was not a writer, she introduced me to her friend, author Gus Russo (*The Outfit, Supermob, Brothers in Arms*, and more), who has now also become my good friend. Gus worked so hard helping me organize my thoughts and write this book. Gus, you are truly a wonderful person and I'm very proud to know you. Thanks, Antoinette, for putting us together, and for all your support and love.

Next, back in Jacksboro, Dianna Brooks Chapman, my dearest and best friend since we were twelve years old, researched many pictures for the book. I'll always love you, Dianna. Mary Pat Carr and Jerry Sharp at the Campbell County Historical Society also were a huge help in researching the early days in LaFollette. Librarians Polly Nodine and Sara Saunders at the Carter Library quickly located my oval office photos and delivered them immediately. In Las Vegas, UNLV Special Collections Librarian Su Kim Chung and her assistant Riva Churchill cheerfully went beyond the call of duty to retrieve hard-to-locate archival information, details that helped put my hazy memories in the correct order. It goes without saying that any errors of fact that remain are mine alone, but all these people did their best to help me get it right. Last, but not least, Brendan Kennedy, of B&K Design in Baltimore, contributed a wonderful interior design and layout, after restoring dozens of damaged photos. I couldn't believe my eyes when I saw what he had done with the boxes of blurry old photos I sent. Thanks a bunch, Brendan, for your incredible attention to detail!

CPSIA information can be obtained at www.ICGtesting.com
Printed in the USA
BVOW101337260613

324367BV00004B/6/P